FRENCH

COMFORT

FOOD

FRENCH
COMFORT
FOOD

HILLARY DAVIS
photographs by STEVEN ROTHFELD

GIBBS SMITH
TO ENRICH AND INSPIRE HUMANKIND

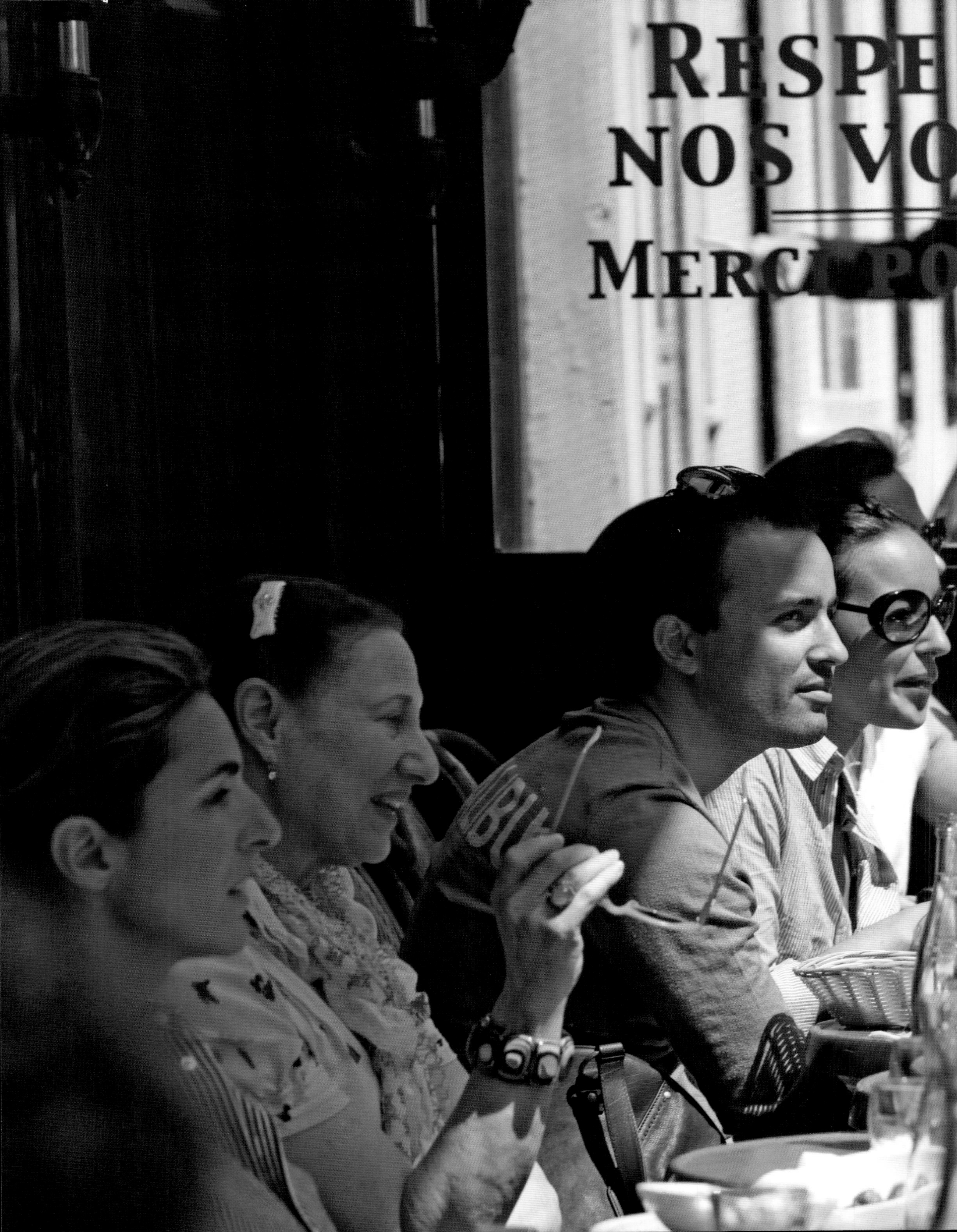
RESPE
NOS VO
MERC

First Edition
18 17 16 15 14   5 4 3 2

Published by
Gibbs Smith
P.O. Box 667
Layton, Utah 84041

1.800.835.4993 orders
www.gibbs-smith.com

Designed by Sheryl Dickert
Printed and bound in Hong Kong

Also by Hillary Davis
Cuisine Niçoise: Sun-Kissed Cooking From The French Riviera
A Million A Minute

Gibbs Smith books are printed on either recycled, 100% post-consumer waste, FSC-certified
papers or on paper produced from sustainable PEFC-certified forest/controlled wood source.
Learn more at www.pefc.org.

Library of Congress Cataloging-in-Publication Data
Davis, Hillary, 1952-
  French comfort food / Hillary Davis ; photographs by Steven Rothfeld. — First edition.
    pages cm
  Includes index.
  ISBN 978-1-4236-3698-4
  1. Cooking, French. 2. Comfort food. I. Title.
  TX719.D2853 2014
  641.5944—dc23
                        2014003084

CONTENTS

❦

INTRODUCTION

If one could describe heaven, for me it would be having a meal in a French restaurant and being able to have all my favorite dishes. There would be an intoxicating fragrance curling up towards my nose, a warmth spreading through me with each bite, a glow from the wine that I drink, a lack of a care in the world while I drag great hunks of warmed baguette through the most amazing sauces and devour each one, and it would have a generous dose of nostalgia. As a result, I would feel content and very happy. The only thing that could make it better would be sharing it with friends and loved ones.

This is what I call comfort food, heavenly when it is good, and totally satisfying.

Some of the best comfort food is French, and it is not that hard to make at home. In fact, many of the dishes are ones French families make every day because they are economical, hearty, and easy to prepare. Yearning for meatballs or shepherd's pie? The French have their own versions. Beef stew over noodles? The French have a recipe for that, too. Mac and Cheese? Yes, again! Paul Bocuse's recipe for *gratin de macaronis* has become a hugely popular recipe that French families make at home—minus the truffles! And when we get to desserts, well, there's nothing quite as satisfying as dipping your spoon into a big bowl of dark chocolate mousse then running your finger along the inside of the bowl to capture every last bit, snacking on *éclairs*, or delving into a rich *tarte Tatin* covered with warm melted caramel sauce.

I would go so far as to say that the French raise the bar on comfort food as we know it. They take mashed potatoes to a whole other level by whipping it with melted cheese to make a dish called *aligot*. They grill ham and cheese sandwiches, but then go one step further and top them with an egg that you pierce so it drips down over the cheese and ham in luscious rivulets.

There are dishes in every region of France that stand out as superb soul-soothers, the ones you would reach for on a gloomy day that are not well-known and not easily found in cookbooks. There's the ancient dish, *crespéou,* a stunning vegetable omelet cake standing high on a plate surrounded by a glorious sauce you swipe your fork through. Or the potato, bacon, and melted cheese wonder from the alpine region of Savoy called *tartiflette.* What could be better than watching snowflakes fall while you tip your fork into this meltingly delicious casserole? Quite possibly, it could be another heartwarming, rich tasting casserole found in southwest France, called *cassoulet,* made with sausages and beans and duck. Once I tasted it, I fell in love and found myself searching for it in restaurants wherever I went. Now I have a way of cooking this labor-intensive dish at home in a slow cooker, and have included the recipe for you to try for yourself. And what about *riz à l'Impératrice,* a luscious rice pudding made with fruit; all the Normandy cider-apples-and-cream dishes; or Brittany's butter cakes and cookies; French Alpine fondues; Alsatian quiches; Burgundy's *bœuf bourguignon* and garlicy escargots; or the sun-drenched Midi's much-loved fish soups and vegetable *tians?*

When I travel throughout France, I always read the menus of restaurants I pass by. When I spy dishes *à l'ancienne* (made the old-fashioned way), *grand-mère* (made the way grandmother made it), or *en croûte* (baked in a buttery crust—I love anything wrapped in dough and baked), I walk in. I know I'll find the kind of dishes I yearn for, cooked in glossy earthenware and served in shiny copper pots, the kind of dishes that have no ambition other than to please the eye and warm the heart. If I'm delighted by a

dish, I write down my impressions about how I think it might be made in my notebook, or I ask the chef if I can have guidance on how to make it.

The friends and acquaintances I've made over the years while living in France enjoy cooking and have been hospitable in sharing with me recipes handed down from their mothers and grandmothers and great-grandmothers—as well as their modern family remakes of the originals. Some of the recipes are nothing more than memories on paper, captured words that their mother used, like "a little of this," "a pinch of that," "then bake until done." I have always collected family recipes wherever I have traveled or lived, because it's my way of discovering the essence of a country, through its people and their food.

So with these resources, plus referring to my hundreds of well-worn cookbooks, I have brought together within these pages my favorite comfort food recipes from France. I hope they will inspire and charm you, reminding you of just how fabulous good home-cooked food from France can be. Come join me at the table! *À table!* ❧

THE FLAVORS OF FRANCE

The comfort foods found in the different regions of France may not be well-known or even made in the rest of the country because of each area having a different climate or geography, but also because some are located on a border with another country where culinary influences produce a cuisine that is a blend of the two cultures.

In Alsace, for example, which is in the northeastern part of France sharing borders with Germany and Switzerland, the cuisine is French with a predominantly German accent. Having been shuffled back and forth between France and Germany as a possession so many times, Alsace developed its own particular flavor of cooking that is not typical of home cooking in the rest of France. To experience the cuisine of Alsace, one must either go there or go to Paris, where Alsatian brasseries sprung up at the end of the nineteenth century when Germany annexed Alsace and so many of its residents moved to Paris to open restaurants like the ones at home. Brasseries became extremely popular and remain so today, beautifully decorated in lavish Art Nouveau or Belle Epoque style and celebrating the region's most beloved dishes.

Typical recipes made in homes and restaurants in Alsace are rustic and simple, cooked in earthenware or copper, often served on folkloric hand-painted plates, some of the most coveted tableware and cookware coming from the clay-rich village of Soufflenheim. They are dark blue and decorated with hand-painted white flowers. There's even a traditional clay pot from Soufflenheim that is used to make sauerkraut or *baeckeoffe*. Meals in Alsace will be served with German-style wines like Riesling, Gewurztraminer, and Sylvaner, poured into iconic tall wine glasses with emerald green goblets.

From *flammekueche*, a thin-crusted pizza with onions and cheese; to *choucroute garnie*, a mountainous pile of sauerkraut, sausages, frankfurters, smoked pork, smoked ham, and boiled potatoes; to chicken cooked in Riesling wine; to baeckeoffe, the multi-layered meat and potato stew cooked in a special oval earthenware dish; to the double-crusted substantial meat pies; to the buttery sweet *kugelhopf* cake baked in its own earthenware mold; to the spiced *leckerli* cookies devoured during the Christmas season—all speak their own language reflective of a culinary culture specific only to the region and its history.

Another border region with its own style of cuisine is along the Côte d'Azur, which snuggles up to the Italian border and the sprawling city of Genoa. Because the region was part of Italy until as recently as 1860, when it was ceded to France, its style of cooking is referred to as cuisine *Niçoise*, a unique blend of French and Italian cooking. The style of cooking is also a result of its particular climate and geography. With little room for cattle to roam due to being located in a narrow area between the Mediterranean Sea and the mountains, dairy products such as butter and cream are largely absent from many of the region's dishes. And because olive trees grow in abundance, olive oil is preferred over butter.

Cuisine Niçoise's signature dishes, like *socca*, the thin chickpea crepe cooked on a huge crepe pan then baked in a wood burning oven; or *tout nus*, meatballs made with spinach, rice, and ground meat; or *barba-jouan*, little fried ravioli stuffed with pumpkin, rice, and Parmesan; *merda de can*, Swiss chard gnocchi; *fada riquet*, savory rice with spinach and cheese; *daube Niçoise*, beef and wine stew flavored with orange peel; *estocaficada*, a heady salt cod stew; *crespéou*, the stacked omelet cake made in the Alps high above the Côte d'Azur; or *tourte de blettes sucrée*, a sweet tart made with Swiss chard, are rarely found once you leave the region, while its other dishes like *pan bagnat*, *salade niçoise*, or *mesclun*, which were invented in Nice, are enjoyed throughout France. Meals cooked at home and in restaurants along the Côte d'Azur will most likely be served on local faïence pottery dishes and water and wine served in hand-blown glasses from the village of Biot.

In the southwest corner of France where the Pyrénées border Spain, French food has a decidedly Spanish accent. This is the Basque region, once its own country called the Kingdom of Navarre until the sixteenth century when Spain invaded it and it then was divided between Spain and France. Almost twenty percent of the people who live in the French side are fluent in the traditional Basque language as well as in French and Spanish.

Because it is located both on the Atlantic Ocean and inland in the mountains, Basque cuisine is abundant in both seafood and meat dishes as well as dishes totally unique due to its history. There's the superb lightly smoked ham, *jambon de Bayonne*; *piperade*, the green peppers, onions, scrambled eggs, and smoked ground red pepper dish; a fabulous cherry soup called *gerezi beltza arno gorriakin*; *pintxos*, little tapas-style dishes served at most bars; *biperrak makallaoz beteta*, pequillo peppers stuffed with salt cod; the thick fish stew made with tuna, peppers, tomatoes, and onions called *marmitako*; and the amazing almond flour cake with pastry cream or cherries called *gâteau Basque*. It is a cuisine that celebrates every form of peppers, from fresh to pickled, to dried, and the entire village of Espelette devotes itself to producing the ground smoky pepper that goes into the making of the hams from Bayonne.

Then, in northwest France, if you stood on a bluff along Brittany's windswept coast, you might hear bagpipes—it has that much of a British vibe. Although not on a border, Brittany is unlike any other region in France due to its history and culture as one of the seven Celtic nations where the people are descended from the original Celtic tribes who emigrated from England to Brittany and made it their home. It has this in common with Scotland, Cornwall, Wales, and Ireland. Its music is even reminiscent of Irish music and its landscape has hints of the English countryside.

Inhabiting a massive peninsula stretching out into the Atlantic Ocean, Brittany has a wealth of fresh seafood and shellfish in its cuisine. It is the major supplier of shellfish, mainly oysters and

mussels, to the rest of France, and a major supplier of natural sea salt to France and the rest of the world. Typical dishes include Breton fish soup, *soupe de poisson*; huge platters piled with shellfish including the Belon oyster, *fruits de mer*; a fish and shellfish stew called *cotriade*; and for sweets, the glazed cake, *kouign-amann*; and a dense custard tart made with prunes called *far Breton*. Crêperies are everywhere, many decorated with lace curtains and displaying local faïence de Quimper plates on the walls, serving sweet crêpes with butter, sugar, and lemon, as well as large savory *galettes* made with buckwheat flour and all sorts of fillings.

In neighboring Normandy, massive cows brought there by the Vikings over 1,000 years ago roam the gently undulating hills of the Pays d'Auge region, munching on grass where sea dew settles every morning. The rich cream and milk delivered by its bovine herds are used to make some of the best butter in France and some of the most popular high-cream cheeses, including Neufchâtel, Pont l'Évêque, Livarot, Camembert, and cream cheeses like Petit-Suisse.

Fresh cream and butter are used in a majority of dishes. Even the fish get a cream bath. *Sole Normande* is created with cream and with fish caught off the fishing village of Honfleur, not far away from this area of thatched-roof cottages, apple orchards, and restaurants decorated with copper pots. In fact, most comforting dishes from Normandy include almost anything paired with cream and butter, including a creamy fish stew called *marmite dieppoise*; and, of course, mussels in cream; baked apples and cream tart, *tarte normande*; rice pudding and

shortbread cookies; and anything in a Vallée d'Auge cream sauce.

In the area surrounding Paris, regional culinary delights include Brie de Meaux cheese; *Chantilly*, whipped cream; an almond cake called *pithiviers*; the Parisian baguette; and *croque-monsieur* and *croque-madame*, grilled cheese sandwiches. However, since the finest produce from all over France is shipped to Paris every day, the cuisine reflects an abundance of what normally would be regional ingredients being used to create dishes, allowing Parisian chefs and home cooks to make almost anything they desire.

Many golden dining memories for me emanate from just north of Paris from the area where Champagne is produced. But rather than recipes, it is the products of the region that I find most comforting. Consider Champagne when things are gloomy! Or the delicate pale pink ladyfingers from Reims to dunk in your Champagne? And what about a slice of soft and creamy Chaource cheese spread on your bread?

Just west of Paris, the Loire River valley is home to magnificent châteaux nestled onto fertile land. The climate is mild, perfect for vineyards and for making the white wines, Muscadet and Sancerre. Typical dishes and products you find there include pork *rillettes*, a spreadable *pâté*; pork cooked with local Vouvray wine, cream, and prunes called *noisettes de porc aux pruneaux de Tours*; the famous *beurre blanc* sauce; dishes made with Cointreau, which is produced in Angers; Guignolet, the cherry liqueur; and a cream cheese called *crémet*.

A majority of *champignons de Paris*, those wonderful little white button mushrooms that dot so many homey stews, are grown here in the Saumur part of the Loire Valley. I remember dining in a side-street restaurant in Paris once and ordering a salad that I'll never forget. It was made simply of sliced *champignons de Paris*, ham, and a Swiss cheese—which were all cut into identical-size matchsticks—tossed in vinaigrette. It is called *salade parisienne*, a delicious mushroom-focused salad I now frequently make in my own home.

In the Poitou-Charentes-Limousin region, below the Loire on the culinary map of France, seafood of the highest quality, such as the famous Marennes claires oysters, and mussels, come from a coastal exposure to the Atlantic, while just inland, highly prized Limousin cattle graze. Poitou-Charentes is also known for its extraordinary butter and cream, and for producing cognac.

The Aquitaine region—whose capital is Bordeaux, one of the most famous wine growing regions in the world—also encompasses the Basque country, Gascony, and the Périgord. With close proximity to the

Atlantic, raw seafood platters and a variety of fish dishes appear in Bordeaux homes and restaurants as much as meats served with the rich *Bordelaise* sauce, named for the city. In Gascony and Périgord, you travel into *foie gras* land, where ducks and geese and truffles become the focus of family dishes and New Year's Eve celebration meals.

One of my all-time favorite meals has to be *bœuf bourguignon* from the Burgundy region of France. I love this wine-soaked beef stew so much that I bought an Emile Henry covered Dutch oven to make it in, which I thought appropriate because the family-owned company is located in Burgundy and uses the surrounding mineral-rich clay of the region to make its cookware. I also love the local specialties of garlicky escargots, *escargots de Bourgogne*; chicken in wine, *coq au vin*; a deeply satisfying dish of eggs poached in Burgundy wine and served on garlic croutons, *œufs en meurette*; miniature playful cheese puffs called *gougères*; ham in parsley jelly, *jambon persillé*; amazing cheeses including Époisses, Mont d'Or, Bleu de Bresse, and Abbaye de Cîteaux; and products, including Dijon mustards. The region is

home to Charolais cattle, aristocratic Bresse poultry, snails, and fresh water fish, as well as some of the finest and oldest vineyards in France. A predominantly wine-based cuisine, it is fully reflective of the *terroir*, with recipes devised to go well with wines from Burgundy that are known for their distinct personality.

To the right side of Burgundy, in the Franche-Comté, they raise cattle, so that's where dried and smoked meats and sausages as well as great cheeses like Morbier and Comté go into the cooking. Doesn't this sound amazing as a snack or lunch: a *croûte au Morbier*, where a slice of farmhouse bread is soaked in white wine then topped with a thick slice of Morbier cheese and baked until melted? Or how about their *michon*? It's like a large flat cheese pancake with a batter made from flour, salt, water, and Comté cheese. Or for a main course, a *poularde aux morilles*, a specialty of the mountainous Jura region made with chicken, vin jaune (yellow wine), and locally picked morel mushrooms served over noodles or soft polenta? Are you hungry yet?

Due south in the Rhône-Alpes region and around the city of Lyon, the tradition of *les Mères Lyonnaises* ensures the ultimate in French homey cooking remains alive and well and available for all in its restaurants and *bouchons* (restaurants serving traditional Lyonnaise dishes). It all goes back to the French revolution, when women, who had been cooks for grand houses in the Lyon area, struck out to start their own businesses feeding the public. Their style of cooking celebrated flavor and local products, and became known as France's cozy hearth of comfort food.

Rather than meticulously planned food that is detailed in presentation, this style of cooking is entirely conjured up based on what is in the garden,

boudin
Noir à
Loignon
Maison

Pieds
et
Paquets
cuisinés
Maison

or based on something found in the farmers' market that morning, or on what is coming into season. Contrary to France's haute cuisine culture that has been primarily dominated by men, this region, with the tradition of les Mères Lyonnaises and their tremendous influence on French bourgeoisie cooking, has been dominated by women. Because of this, many refer to Lyon as the culinary capital of France. Regional dishes—ham with lentils, *petit salé*; fish dumplings with Nantua sauce, named after Nantua lake, *quenelles*; *salade lyonnaise*; *andouillette* sausages; all the meats and cured pork dishes from the farms in the west of the region, including pigs' feet, rosette sausages, and beautiful pâtés and terrines have become favorites of French families in the entire country.

As you drive up hairpin turns into the French Alps, houses become chalets, hills become steeper, and the cooking progressively becomes more robust and filling. The region is known as the Savoie, where potato and cheese dishes are served in romantic settings before a fireplace while snow squalls whirl outside. It's the kind of food you dream of when it is cold and icy and gray. At country inns or *auberges*, *diots*, sausages cooked in wine, are brought to the table along with mountain bread and mustard. Perhaps next would be a *tartiflette*. At the highest summit of the comfort-food mountain, this dish has a base of potatoes, bacon, onions, and cream then is baked with great slabs of local Reblochon cheese which melts all over the top. Another table in the restaurant may be offered warm mulled wine to start off the evening followed by a cheese fondue laced with Kirsch, garlic, and white wine served in a shallow round ceramic pot over a flame with long forks to spear hunks of bread to dip into the melted cheese.

There's also my favorite, gratin *savoyard*, which is like a gratin *dauphinois*, except with the addition of eggs and cheese. This is where Génépy des Alpes is made, a liqueur infused with Alpine herbs. And it is where the much sought after pottery from the Lake Annecy area is made, the one with a polka dot pattern representing the harvest moon over the lake.

At the center of the country, in the Auvergne and Limousin regions, they also have their own regional comforting dishes, including a hearty *potée*, a thick cabbage soup; the delicious vanilla-scented dessert called *flognarde*; *truffade,* a bacon, potato, and cheese casserole; *clafoutis*, baked flans with black cherries; and cheeses the French love to present on their cheese boards, including the creamy Bleu d'Auvergne, Fourme d'Ambert, and Cantal, all eminently pleasing to the palette and to the soul.

In the south, in the Languedoc and in sun-drenched Provence, favorite dishes may be served on local Moustiers faïence pottery and be cooked in earthenware *tians* and *daubières*. Residents in this region are blessed with an abundance of fresh produce, from vegetables to melons, citrus, Camargue rice, almonds, and olives. Herbs are scavenged wild along hillside roads to scent their dishes. Favorite family recipes include braised artichokes, *artichauts à la barigoule*; a confectionary called *calissons;* fish stew, *bouillabaisse*; vegetable soup with basil and garlic, *soupe au pistou*; a puffy pastry filled with vanilla cream, *tarte tropézienne*; a flat bread, *fougasse*; a sauce made with egg yolks, garlic, and olive oil, *aïoli*; an olive spread called tapenade; puréed salt cod with garlic, *brandade de morue*; and a white fish stew, *bourride*.

In France, restaurants and home cooks take pride in preserving the recipes of their regional heritage and deeply rooted traditions. From haute cuisine, to the ultra-light cuisine *minceur*, to minimalism, to whatever trend that passes through, what has remained true over time in French homes and small village restaurants is a determination to hold onto their beloved regional classic dishes, the ones they grew up with that their mothers and grandmothers and grandmothers before them made. These are the ones they return to when they are on vacation, the ones they share with friends on weekends, cook for their families, and reward a birthday with. The comfort food of France is all about nostalgia and about food that brings back happy memories.

Why is a passion for food so important to the French, no matter what region they live in?

Whether in residential neighborhoods in big cities or in medieval villages in the rural countryside, families, on a day-to-day basis, put thought into and take care in preparing food and wine as a way of celebrating life. It is a state of mind that is deeply infused into the collective psyche.

They wake up thinking about food. They buy a freshly baked loaf of bread every morning, plan what they want to cook that day while they commute to work, shop with a keen eye, and prepare their daily meals with pride. They can spend hours strolling through weekend open-air markets, deciding their weekend menu based on what they see and what is in season. As their lives are becoming faster and faster paced, cooking is a way of returning to and reconnecting with a cherished, slower way of life for a little while in the kitchen and around the family table.

A love for cooking at home is not only a state of mind—it is a form of entertainment—something they take pleasure in. If they have time, they delight in the finer details of menu creation and table art. If they whip something up on the spur of the moment, it is again with enjoyment, confident that their cupboards are well stocked with treats they have accumulated over the year on their travels—olive oil from a small orchard in the south of France, piment d'Espelette from the village of Espelette, a box of tiny lentils from Le Puy.

Parties at home are focused on food, and any chance to celebrate is taken; holidays, weeknight dinner parties, birthdays, or just to be able to invite friends and family to sit at a wooden table in the backyard to dine under the stars.

Above all, celebrating the foods of their region, valuing the meaning of keeping tradition alive, and sharing it with those they love with the intent to please is exactly what makes French home cooking so comforting and so beloved to the rest of us. ✳

WELCOMING STARTERS AND SAVORY NIBBLES

The French excel at setting the scene for a meal.

Even if the family is running in all directions and only comes together for weekend meals or when friends come over, those meals they share around a table at home have a traditional way of unfolding. The table is set and candles lit. A sprig of herbs or a small flower from the garden may be placed beside each napkin, a reflection of the time of year or simply to provide a spontaneous simple decoration. The mood slows down, conversation starts, wine is opened, and children gather in the kitchen to help bring plates to the table. There's always a first course, an opening act that is meant to be a treat or to delight.

The most touching example of this was a lunch I had with friends at their home in the south of France. When we sat down, there were three appetizers displayed family-style on platters down the center of the table, all a surprise for me because they were prepared from recipes in my cookbook, *Cuisine Niçoise*.

Another tradition is to relax for a while before even thinking of sitting at the table, for *l'heure de l'apéro*, the French cocktail hour. Especially on Saturdays, it's a time when friends *rendez-vous* at a café for wine and conversation and nibbles like potato chips, olives, or peanuts. When *l'apéro* is taken at home with friends, the snacks and nibbles can become a buffer while waiting for dinner to be served and are substantially more interesting and fun.

CHEESE SOUFFLÉS IN A MUG

Petits Soufflés au Fromage SERVES 8

In a restaurant in Paris many years ago, I was served my first soufflé. It was a magnificently puffed vanilla one with a dusting of powdered sugar. Horrified, I watched the waiter attack its center with two large silver serving spoons, deflating it almost immediately. He then poured in a generous amount of Grand Marnier, smiled, and served me a portion. The center was creamy and sweet and so pungent with the orange liqueur that it brought tears to my eyes. I loved it. Ever since, I have made soufflés, both sweet and savory, and it's a frequent dish at my table.

This savory cheese soufflé recipe is super easy to make and there's enough for a group of 8—or for 4 people to have seconds. It makes a wonderful appetizer or light lunch with salad. Just turn over your cups or mugs and check that they are oven proof.

SPECIAL EQUIPMENT PASTRY BRUSH; 8 (8-OUNCE / 225-ML) OVEN-PROOF MUGS, CUPS, OR RAMEKINS; ROASTING PAN OR LARGE BAKING PAN; MEDIUM SAUCEPAN; STAND MIXER

4 tablespoons (½ stick / 60 g) unsalted butter, plus 1 tablespoon melted butter

¼ cup (40 g) seasoned breadcrumbs

8 large eggs, room temperature

4 tablespoons (30 g) all-purpose flour

1½ cups (350 ml) milk

1 teaspoon salt

dash cayenne pepper

1 teaspoon Dijon mustard

6 ounces (170 g) Comté cheese, grated (about 1½ cups)

½ teaspoon cream of tartar

PREP

With the pastry brush, spread the melted butter inside of the mugs, starting at the bottom and brushing with upward strokes towards the lip. Coat the insides of the cups with breadcrumbs all the way up to the lip, tap out excess, and place mugs in the refrigerator until ready to use.

Preheat oven to 400° F (200° C) and place roasting pan filled with an inch of boiling water on the middle rack of the oven.

Separate the eggs into whites and yolks, discarding 1 of the egg yolks so that you have 7 egg yolks and 8 egg whites. Make sure there is no yolk in the egg whites.

COOK

Melt 4 tablespoons (60 g) butter in saucepan to make a béchamel sauce. Whisk in the flour and continue whisking on low heat for 1 minute. Slowly pour in half the milk while you whisk then add the rest of the milk and whisk until the sauce thickens and starts bubbling. Add the salt, cayenne, mustard, and cheese and stir to mix. Remove the sauce from the heat and cool to room temperature.

In a large bowl, whisk 7 egg yolks until pale yellow. Whisk them into the béchamel sauce.

In a very clean dry bowl of the stand mixer, whip the egg whites and cream of tartar until they hold their shape. Don't over beat; you want more billowy

continued >

mounds than stiff peaks. Use a rubber spatula to gently fold third of the egg whites into the egg yolk mixture then fold in the rest without deflating them. Spoon the mixture into the mugs up to the rim. Run your thumb around the inside of the rim of each mug to help the soufflés rise in the center.

Place the mugs in the roasting pan in the oven and bake for about 12 minutes. Do not open the oven door while they are baking, but do turn on the oven light and peak through the glass to see how they are doing after 11 minutes.

Remove from the oven when they are fully puffed up and golden. Serve immediately because the soufflés will begin to deflate after a few minutes.

IDEAS AND SUBSTITUTIONS

If you have elegant coffee or teacups that are oven proof (fine porcelain is not meant for the oven), they are great for making these little soufflés for formal occasions.

Comté is a mild French cheese with a subtle flavor. If you would like a more pronounced cheese flavor, use a sharp cheddar or any of your favorite cheeses. And if you don't want to use breadcrumbs to coat the cups, use flour or grated Parmesan cheese instead to give the soufflés something to "climb" as they rise.

The restaurant where I had my first soufflé still exists if you are visiting Paris. Le Soufflé can be found at 36 Rue Mont Thabor.

LIGHT AND CRISPY FISH FINGERS WITH RÉMOULADE DIPPING SAUCE

Goujonnettes de Poisson, Sauce Rémoulade SERVES 4

I like deep or shallow frying everything in olive oil for the extra flavor it gives. This recipe is for a light French version of fish fingers, elegant enough to serve as an appetizer or to heap on a silver platter and pass with sauce at a gathering.

SPECIAL EQUIPMENT STAND MIXER OR HAND-HELD ELECTRIC MIXER; PARCHMENT PAPER; MEDIUM HEAVY SKILLET

Rémoulade Dipping Sauce

2 tablespoons (20 g) capers

4 cornichons (or tiny dill pickles)

2 sprigs fresh tarragon

½ cup (120 ml) vegetable oil

½ cup (120 ml) extra virgin olive oil

2 egg yolks, room temperature

2 teaspoons Dijon mustard

¼ teaspoon salt

½ teaspoon sugar

1 tablespoon (15 ml) white wine or tarragon vinegar

Fish

¾ cup (90 g) all-purpose flour

½ teaspoon salt

8 cracks freshly ground black pepper

¼ teaspoon cayenne pepper

¼ teaspoon turmeric

4 large eggs, room temperature

1 cup (150 g) seasoned breadcrumbs

1½ pounds (680 g) fresh flounder, sliced diagonally in 1-inch (2.5 cm) slices

1 cup (240 ml) olive oil, plus more if you are using a large skillet

2 lemons, quartered

PREP FOR SAUCE

Finely chop capers, cornichons, and leaves from the sprigs tarragon and mix together. Discard tarragon stems. Mix vegetable oil and olive oil together.

PREP FOR FISH

Place the flour on a plate. Add the salt, pepper, cayenne, and turmeric and mix well with a fork. Beat the eggs in a large shallow bowl and place next to the plate with flour. Place a plate with the breadcrumbs next to the eggs.

Preheat oven to 300° F (150° C).

COOK

Sauce

Place the egg yolks, mustard, salt, and sugar in the bowl of the stand mixer and beat until pale yellow and thick, about 1 minute. While beating, begin to slowly drip in the mixed oils until you achieve the consistency of mayonnaise. Beat in the vinegar. Stir in the capers, cornichons, and tarragon.

Fish

Roll the pieces of flounder in the flour, shake off excess, dip into beaten eggs, and then roll in the breadcrumbs. Lay them on piece of parchment paper, and when that fills up, lay another piece of parchment paper on top and continue to add pieces of breaded flounder.

Heat olive oil to 360° F (180° C) in the skillet then shallow-fry the fish, a few at a time, for about 30 seconds each side until golden brown. Drain on paper towels and keep warm in the oven, if you wish. Serve with the Rémoulade Dipping Sauce and lemon wedges.

IDEAS AND SUBSTITUTIONS

Alongside the fish fingers, you can serve French fries for dipping as well.

KNITTING NEEDLE SPIRALS WITH PISTOU

Spirals au Pistou MAKES 24 (6-INCH / 15-CM) SPIRALS

Whether you neatly stack them like logs or heap them in a pile like pick-up-sticks, these crunchy little puff pastry spirals are the perfect accompaniment for wine at l'heure de l'apéro—*that point in the day when work is done, the light turns golden, and evening is just beginning.*

The first time I made them, from a picture in a French magazine, I couldn't get the shape right. So I played with my knitting needles and came up with a way to produce the lovely spirals. I've filled mine with pistou, *the Niçoise version of Italian pesto. As the spirals bake, the scent of basil, garlic, and cheese fills the kitchen and lingers until the guests arrive.*

SPECIAL EQUIPMENT FOOD PROCESSOR; ROLLING PIN; PIZZA CUTTER; 1 KNITTING NEEDLE, #11–#15, OR A CHOPSTICK; 2 BAKING SHEETS LINED WITH PARCHMENT PAPER

5 ounces (140 g) Parmesan cheese, plus ½ cup (45 g) grated

4 large cloves garlic

1 cup (50 g) tightly packed fresh basil leaves

¼ teaspoon salt

2 dashes cayenne pepper

3 tablespoons (45 ml) extra virgin olive oil, plus more to grease knitting needle

1 sheet frozen puff pastry, thawed

coarsely ground black pepper, to taste

PREP

Slice the 5 ounces (140 g) of Parmesan. Preheat oven to 375° F (190° C).

COOK

Pistou

Toss the garlic, sliced Parmesan, basil, salt, and cayenne in a food processor and process for 10 seconds. With the machine running, slowly pour in 3 tablespoons (45 ml) olive oil until the mixture becomes a spreadable paste.

Spirals

Lightly flour a clean work surface and unfurl the pastry sheet on it. With the rolling pin, roll out the pastry until it is 12 inches (30 cm) long. Thickly spread the Pistou over the bottom half of the rectangle, leaving a ¼-inch (6-mm) border on the left, bottom, and right sides. Fold over the top half to cover the bottom half. Using your thumbs, press down all the way around the edges to seal.

Sprinkle the surface with grated Parmesan and black pepper. Gently press down with your fingers then, with the rolling pin, roll up and down until the rectangle is 12 inches (30 cm) long. Using the pizza cutter, cut crosswise into ½-inch (1.5-cm) strips then cut again vertically to make 6-inch (15-cm) long strips.

Grease the knitting needle with olive oil and loosely wind one of the strips around and around the needle. Slide it off onto a baking sheet. Press the top of the spiral into the baking sheet to secure it, gently stretch out the spiral and press at the other end. Continue until all the spirals are made.

Bake for 9–11 minutes, until golden. Cool to room temperature before serving.

IDEAS AND SUBSTITUTIONS

If you have any Pistou leftover, freeze it and use as a topping for pasta.

RAMEKINS OF CHILLED TUNA AND CAPER SPREAD

Rillettes de Thon aux Câpres SERVES 4–6

Rillettes are small spreadable pâtés *that can be made from meat, poultry, or seafood with some kind of fat which is then spread on bread or crackers. Take them on picnics, offer a couple of them on the table for appetizers, or have one or two with small toasts and wine.*

SPECIAL EQUIPMENT STAND MIXER; MEDIUM SERVING BOWL OR INDIVIDUAL RAMEKINS

1 organic lemon

1 tablespoon (10 g) capers in brine

2 (6-ounce / 170-g) cans best-quality tuna in olive oil

½ (2-ounce / 60-g) can anchovies in oil

7 wedges Laughing Cow Creamy Swiss cheese, room temperature

2 tablespoons (30 ml) extra virgin olive oil

1 tablespoon Dijon mustard

4 cracks freshly ground black pepper

1 large shallot, peeled and finely chopped

2 tablespoons finely chopped parsley

PREP

Wash the lemon, juice it, and grate the zest on a box grater. Drain the capers and coarsely chop, reserving some whole ones for garnish. Drain tuna and anchovies then squeeze in paper towels to dry.

COOK

In the stand mixer, blend the tuna and anchovies. Add the cheese, olive oil, lemon juice, 1 tablespoon grated lemon zest, mustard, and pepper and mix well. Stir in the shallot, chopped capers, and parsley. Taste for seasoning.

Spoon into serving bowl or ramekins and garnish with whole capers.

IDEAS AND SUBSTITUTIONS

You can make this up to 2 days ahead and bring to room temperature before serving. Dill or tarragon can be substituted for the parsley.

PATE AUX PATATES

9,90 €

Saveurs & Traditions

RAMEKINS OF WARM SALMON, WINE, AND SHALLOTS

Rillettes de Saumon, Beurre Blanc Nantais SERVES 4

Based on the classic French dish, Salmon with Beurre Blanc Nantais, *this* rillette *is dressed and ready to make an elegant entrance to any gathering.*

SPECIAL EQUIPMENT SMALL SAUCEPAN; STAND MIXER; MEDIUM SERVING BOWL OR INDIVIDUAL RAMEKINS

3 large shallots, peeled and finely chopped

½ teaspoon salt

4 tablespoons (60 ml) white wine vinegar, plus ½ teaspoon

½ cup (120 ml) Muscadet wine (or dry white wine)

8 tablespoons (120 g) unsalted butter, room temperature, plus extra for salmon

2 teaspoons fresh lemon juice

1½ tablespoons finely chopped fresh tarragon leaves

salt and pepper, to taste

1 pound (450 g) fresh salmon

PREP

Preheat broiler.

COOK

Cook the shallots, salt, 4 tablespoons (60 ml) vinegar, and wine in the saucepan and reduce until there is almost no liquid left. Stir in the butter, a little at a time, on low heat until melted. Sprinkle in remaining vinegar, lemon juice, and tarragon and stir again. Season with salt and pepper.

Dot the salmon with a little butter, salt, and pepper, and broil until just done, for approximately 5 minutes. Transfer to the mixing bowl of stand mixer, flake the salmon with a fork, add the shallot mixture, then beat in the stand mixer for 30 seconds, until combined but the salmon is still in small pieces. Scoop into a serving bowl or ramekins and serve while still warm with toast or crackers.

IDEAS AND SUBSTITUTIONS

Any fish can be substituted for the salmon.

RAMEKINS OF WARM PORK AND APPLES

Rillettes de Porc aux Pommes SERVES 4–6

Normally pork rillettes *means cubes of pork that have been cooked slowly in fat until they become very tender and are mashed into a spread. Instead, I make pulled pork for this recipe and perk up the flavor with tart green apples.*

SPECIAL EQUIPMENT MEDIUM SAUCEPAN; STAND MIXER; MEDIUM SERVING BOWL OR INDIVIDUAL RAMEKINS

1 pound (450 g) pork tenderloin

3 cups (720 ml) chicken stock

2 cloves garlic, pressed

3 tablespoons (45 ml) extra virgin olive oil

6 tablespoons (90 g) unsalted butter, room temperature

1/2 teaspoon salt

8 cracks freshly ground black pepper

2 Granny Smith apples, peeled and diced

PREP

Slice the tenderloin into 3 to 4 pieces.

COOK

In the saucepan, add the stock and pork and bring to a boil. Turn down the heat, skim, turn the pieces of pork over, and reduce to a simmer. Cook for 25 minutes. Transfer the pork to a cutting board and cool to room temperature. Shred the pork using two forks.

To the stand mixer bowl, add the pork, garlic, olive oil, butter, salt, and pepper and beat until combined but still a coarse texture. Taste and add more salt and pepper, if desired. Stir in the apples.

Spoon into a serving dish or ramekins and garnish with coarsely ground black pepper. Serve warm with sliced baguette.

IDEAS AND SUBSTITUTIONS

Try soaking the diced apples in apple brandy or Calvados before folding into the pork mixture, or using freshly diced pears instead of apples.

ESCARGOTS BAKED IN CAMPARI TOMATOES

Escargots Rôtis dans des Tomates Campari SERVES 4

When you are in France, you eat snails. France consumes more snails than anywhere else in the world, mostly in the style they serve them in Burgundy (à la Bourguignonne) with garlic and parsley butter. They are gathered wild in meadows or raised on snail farms, and are available in most supermarkets or gourmet stores.

I serve them tucked into Campari tomatoes, swimming in garlic and parsley butter and baked in a large round shallow dish. I place the dish in the center of the table or counter for guests or family to share. They scoop them up, sometimes with their hands, sometimes with a serving spoon, and enjoy them right then and there, hot out of the oven. Warm hunks of baguette are then dragged through the remaining sauce.

You will most likely only use half of the garlic parsley butter for the escargots, but I always make more for this recipe so that I can either freeze the rest or use it to make garlic bread the next day.

SPECIAL EQUIPMENT SHALLOW BAKING DISH OR 4 INDIVIDUAL GRATIN DISHES; FOOD PROCESSOR; BAKING SHEET OR LARGE BAKING PAN

extra virgin olive oil

24 medium Campari tomatoes

½ bunch parsley

1 baguette

6 medium cloves garlic

1 medium shallot

½ teaspoon salt

1 cup (2 sticks / 230 g) unsalted butter, room temperature

2 cans escargots (24 snails), rinsed and patted dry

salt and freshly ground pepper, to taste

PREP

Generously oil the baking dish or dishes. Clean tomatoes and dry. Slice off tops and remove inside flesh and juices to a bowl. Slice off a little bit on the bottom of each so they sit flat (be careful not to create a hole) and place all in baking dish or 6 in each of gratin dishes. Wash and dry parsley, pull off the leaves, and discard the stems. Slice thick pieces of a fourth of the baguette, cut off crusts, then slice into small cubes. Slice the rest of the baguette.

Preheat oven to 375° F (190° C).

COOK

In the food processor, add the garlic and shallot and process for 15 seconds. Add salt and parsley and process for 5 seconds. Add the butter and process until you have a paste. Spoon a small amount of the garlic butter into the bottom of each tomato, add a snail, and top with another dab of the garlic butter.

Place the baking dish with the tomatoes on the baking sheet and sprinkle salt and pepper over the tops. Scatter the cubes of bread around the baking sheet and pop into the oven for approximately 18 minutes, or until the butter sauce in the tomatoes begins to bubble. However, take the bread cubes out after 6 minutes, or when golden, and place in a serving bowl.

Serve the tomatoes hot with sliced baguette and toasted cubes to the side to soak up the garlic butter sauce.

IDEAS AND SUBSTITUTIONS

You can substitute large mushroom caps for the Campari tomatoes.

TRIO OF PROVENÇAL SPREADS

Trois Tartinades Provençales SERVES 6–8

Tartinade *is a French word for any kind of soft spread, either salty or sweet. I used to buy a variety of them from a stall in Cannes' Forville Market until I learned how to make them at home. I serve three at a time in identical square flat glasses or small serving bowls, have a spoon in each, and crackers or fresh bread on the side.*

They will keep in the refrigerator, with a couple of tablespoons of olive oil on top, for up to 2 weeks.

SPECIAL EQUIPMENT FOOD PROCESSOR

Chickpenade

1 (15-ounce / 420-g) can chickpeas (garbanzo beans), drained

1 cup (125 g) pitted green olives

1 tablespoon (10 g) capers in brine, drained

2 tablespoons (30 ml) fresh lemon juice

¼ cup (60 ml) extra virgin olive oil

1 teaspoon tomato paste

Tomatenade

1 cup (120 g) sun-dried tomatoes in oil, drained

2 cloves garlic

2 tablespoons (20 g) capers in brine, drained

4 large fresh basil leaves

¼ cup (60 ml) extra virgin olive oil

1 tablespoon (15 ml) red wine vinegar

1 teaspoon tomato paste

Poivronade

1 (16-ounce / 450-g) jar roasted red bell peppers, drained

1 fresh hot red pepper, without seeds

3 cloves garlic

1 tablespoon (15 ml) fresh lemon juice

1 tablespoon (10 g) capers in brine, drained

2 tablespoons (30 ml) extra virgin olive oil

2 tablespoons flat-leaf parsley, chopped

COOK

To prepare each tartinade, add the ingredients to the food processor, pulse until you have either a finely minced or smooth consistency, and spread some Provençal sunshine.

INDIVIDUAL CARAMELIZED ONION AND ROQUEFORT CLAFOUTIS

Clafoutis aux Oignons Caramélisés et au Roquefort SERVES 4

Clafoutis are the iconic dessert flans made with black cherries in the Limousin region of France. To make a savory one, you just eliminate the fruit and sugar and add whatever you wish. For this rendition, I've chosen Roquefort, the creamy sharp blue cheese made in caves in southwest France, and caramelized onions.

The AOC (Appellation d'Origine Contrôlée) guarantees the authenticity and quality of a product. As the flagship of French food, Roquefort has the oldest appellation and was the first French cheese to achieve this status in 1925. For a cheese to deserve the Roquefort mark, it must meet stringent specifications including natural and human factors, implying a close link between the product, the land of its production, and the skills of the people living there.

SPECIAL EQUIPMENT 4 (1-CUP / 240-ML) GRATIN DISHES OR RAMEKINS; LARGE SKILLET

- 2 tablespoons (30 g) unsalted butter
- 1 medium onion, cut in half and thinly sliced
- 2 teaspoons sugar
- 3 large eggs, room temperature
- 1 large egg yolk, room temperature
- ½ cup (60 g) all-purpose flour
- ½ cup (120 ml) milk
- ½ cup (120 ml) heavy cream
- freshly ground nutmeg
- ¼ teaspoon salt
- 4 cracks freshly ground pepper
- 4 ounces (110 g) Roquefort, sliced into 4 equal slices
- 1 tablespoon fresh thyme leaves

PREP

Butter the gratin dishes. Preheat the oven to 350° F (180° C).

COOK

In the skillet, melt the butter and cook the onion on medium-low heat until tender, about 8 minutes. Add the sugar, turn up the heat to medium high, and cook until the onions turn golden brown and are caramelized.

Whisk together the eggs, egg yolk, flour, milk, cream, nutmeg, salt, and pepper in a mixing bowl.

Divide the onions in the bottoms of the gratin dishes, add a slice of cheese, gently pour the egg mixture over the top, and sprinkle with the thyme leaves. Bake for about 35 minutes, until golden and puffed. Serve immediately.

IDEAS AND SUBSTITUTIONS

You can substitute the Roquefort with any blue cheese, and the milk and cream with fat-free half-and-half.

Instead of Roquefort and onions, try finely chopped walnuts and thinly sliced pears, mushrooms and cheese, zucchini and cherry tomatoes, figs and goat cheese, shallots and mussels, or bacon and eggs for a breakfast or brunch clafoutis. Pair any of these with a crisp white wine. Trés bon indeed!

NIÇOISE STUFFED VEGETABLES

Petits Farcis Niçois SERVES 4

In the region around Nice in the south of France, they fill miniature vegetables with a meatloaf mixture and call them "petits farcis." It's a favorite snack sold in open-air markets and is offered as appetizers in restaurants. If you can find really small vegetables to stuff, it makes a delightful presentation. If not, just use any vegetables from your garden or farmers' market, and try for a uniform size so they all cook evenly.

SPECIAL EQUIPMENT BAKING DISH LARGE ENOUGH TO HOLD ALL THE VEGETABLES; INSTANT-READ THERMOMETER

4 small onions

4 medium firm tomatoes

2 small to medium zucchini

2 slices bread

1 cup (240 ml) red wine

1 beef or chicken bouillon cube

6 tablespoons (90 ml) extra virgin olive oil, divided, plus extra

4 large cloves garlic, peeled and minced

1 pound (450 g) ground beef

1 pound (450g) ground pork

1 large egg, room temperature, beaten

2 tablespoons tomato paste

1 tablespoon herbes de Provence

2 dashes cayenne pepper

12 cracks freshly ground black pepper

½ cup (75 g) seasoned breadcrumbs

¼ teaspoon salt

PREP

Peel the onions, slice their tops off and keep the lids. With a spoon or grapefruit spoon, remove the insides of the onions so there is room to stuff them. Carefully cut a thin slice off the bottoms so they will "sit" when stuffed. Finely chop the insides and toss into a mixing bowl.

Slice the tops off the tomatoes and keep the lids. Remove the flesh and seeds from the tomatoes and discard. Very carefully slice off a small amount from bottoms of the tomatoes so they "sit" when stuffed. Invert tomatoes and their tops on a paper towel to drain.

Slice the zucchini in half lengthwise. Scoop out enough of the flesh to make room for the stuffing. Discard flesh.

Lay the bread in the wine until soft and soaked through, squeeze dry, then crumble and toss in the bowl with the chopped onion. Reserve the remaining wine.

Lightly grease the baking dish with olive oil and preheat the oven to 400° F (200° C).

COOK

Blanche the onions and their "lids" in boiling water for 5 minutes. Drain on paper towels.

Wrap the bouillon cube in plastic wrap and give it a couple of whacks with a hammer to pulverize it, if needed. Unwrap and shake the powder into 3 tablespoons (45 ml) olive oil and microwave for 50 seconds. Mix well with a fork to dissolve then pour into the bowl.

Add the garlic, beef, pork, egg, tomato paste, herbes de Provence, cayenne, pepper, and breadcrumbs. Mix well with clean hands or a fork. Spoon the mixture into the vegetables, trying not to compact the meat too much. Mound the meat in a high dome on each vegetable and fit them into the baking dish with their lids on.

Whisk remaining olive oil and salt into the remaining wine then pour over the vegetables. Bake for 30 minutes or until the thermometer inserted into the center of a stuffed vegetable reads 145 degrees (62° C) for medium rare or 160 degrees (70° C) for medium. Note: this recipe is for medium to small vegetables. For tiny vegetables the cooking time will be less. Serve hot out of the oven or at room temperature.

IDEAS OR SUBSTITUTIONS

For an end-of-year holiday buffet table, use only red and green vegetables—tomatoes, zucchini, red peppers, and green peppers.

SAVORY TOMATO BASIL CAKE

Cake à la Tomate et au Basilic SERVES 6-8

Made popular by French cookbook author Sophie Dudemaine after she wrote her best-seller, Les Cakes de Sophie, small, savory quick cakes have become a French family favorite because they are flavorful, fast, and easy to create with ingredients on hand.

Tomato, basil, and olive oil are the Provençal ingredients that define this savory loaf from the south of France. Slightly sweet, serve slices or cubes with a smear of salty black olive tapenade or goat cheese and a chilled rosé wine.

SPECIAL EQUIPMENT 9 X 5 X 3-INCH (23 X 13 X 7.5-CM) LOAF PAN; FOOD PROCESSOR

2 medium tomatoes

¼ cup (30 g) sun-dried tomatoes in oil, drained

2 cups (240 g) all-purpose flour

1 tablespoon baking powder

1 teaspoon baking soda

½ teaspoon salt

6 cracks coarsely ground black pepper

1 cup (50 g) tightly packed fresh basil leaves

¾ cup (150 g) sugar

2 tablespoons tomato paste

3 large eggs, room temperature, beaten

6 tablespoons (90 ml) extra virgin olive oil, plus extra

PREP

Preheat oven to 350° F (180° C) and liberally oil the loaf pan.

Quarter then seed the tomatoes and drain on a paper towel. Coarsely chop sun-dried tomatoes and pat off excess oil with paper towels.

COOK

In a large mixing bowl, sift the flour, baking powder, baking soda, salt, and pepper.

In the food processor, add the basil and sugar and process for 5 seconds. Scrape down the sides. Add the tomatoes, tomato paste, eggs, and olive oil. Process for 5 seconds. Pour into the bowl of dry ingredients, toss in the chopped sun-dried tomatoes, and stir with a wooden spoon until just blended. Like making muffins, you don't want to overwork the dough.

Scoop everything into the loaf pan and bake for 40–45 minutes or until golden brown. Cool for 5 minutes then invert the pan onto a plate or wire rack and cool the bread to room temperature before slicing, about 15 minutes.

IDEAS AND SUBSTITUTIONS

You can add or substitute to your heart's content with this basic recipe. Try tiny cubes of ham, cheese, or olives. Also, the cake has a lovely texture using olive oil, but if you would prefer to use butter instead, substitute the 6 tablespoons olive oil with 1 stick (230 g) unsalted butter, at room temperature. Also, try making it in mini-cake molds.

MUSHROOM STEW IN PUFF PASTRY CASES

Vol-au-Vent aux Champignons SERVES 6

The hollows of individual puff pastry shells are filled to overflowing with a fabulous mushroom stew for this small appetizer that is easy to make with ready-made frozen puff pastry (vol-au-vent) shells.

The sauce for the filling is made along the lines of a classic béchamel sauce, but without the butter or milk. I make it with olive oil rather than butter—a flavorful healthy alternative that pairs well with the mushrooms and garlic in this dish. And instead of using milk, I use chicken stock and sherry to lighten it up and layer in more flavors.

SPECIAL EQUIPMENT LARGE SAUCEPAN; LARGE SKILLET

6 frozen ready-to-bake puff pastry shells (vol-au-vent shells)	4 tablespoons (30 g) all-purpose flour	2 large cloves garlic, peeled and minced
½ bunch parsley	1¼ cups (300 ml) chicken stock	1 pound (450 g) mushrooms (button, portobello, or cremini), coarsely chopped
7 tablespoons (10 cl) extra virgin olive oil, divided	¾ cup (180 ml) good quality dry sherry	
1 large shallot, peeled and minced	2 chicken bouillon cubes, finely chopped	1 teaspoon kosher salt
		10 cracks freshly ground black pepper, plus more to garnish

PREP

Bake the pastry shells according to package instructions, being careful to watch and take out when golden. Slice off the stems of the parsley and mince the leaves. Discard stems.

COOK

In the saucepan, heat 4 tablespoons (60 ml) olive oil, add the shallot and cook on medium for 3 minutes. Add the flour and continuously whisk for 3 minutes then very slowly whisk in the stock, sherry, and chopped bouillon cubes and cook until the bouillon cubes are melted and the sauce thickens.

Heat remaining olive oil in the large skillet on medium heat, add the garlic and cook for 2 minutes.

Add the mushrooms (working in 2 batches if your skillet cannot hold all of the mushrooms), salt, and pepper and cook on high for 5 minutes. Transfer all, including any mushroom juice in the skillet, to the saucepan then stir in the parsley.

Evenly divide the mixture, filling the pastry shells. Crack coarsely ground black pepper on top of each and top with their lids at a jaunty angle to serve.

IDEAS AND SUBSTITUTIONS

Use vegetable stock to make a vegetarian version. In addition to mushrooms, chicken and leftover steak or filet mignon go very well in this combination.

BRUNCH FRENCH STYLE

The French don't normally make brunch at home. In fact, they don't really eat very much for breakfast other than perhaps a piece of baguette slathered with butter or a bit of jam, which they call a *tartine.* Or they might stop for a croissant and coffee at the café on the corner on the way to work, or pick up freshly baked pastries on the weekend. Omelets are reserved for lunch or late nights and French toast is eaten as dessert.

However, this most American tradition has firmly taken hold in Paris and other major cities across France, where their cafés, restaurants, and tearooms serve *"le brunch"* on weekends.

The following recipes are dishes that fit perfectly into a French-style brunch you can make at home.

FRENCH TOAST WITH HOMEMADE ORANGE BUTTER

Pain Perdu, Beurre à l'Orange MAKES 8 SLICES AND ½ CUP (120 G) BUTTER

A popular dish in France since the fifteenth century, pain perdu *translates to mean "lost bread"—and is served for dessert or as a sweet afternoon snack. It is the same technique as for making French toast, using day-old bread to soak up an egg custard then cooking it.*

I pair mine with Homemade Orange Butter before drizzling it with maple syrup. The joy in making your own butter is that you can use cream from local farm-raised cows you know graze in open pastures, which ensures a superior tasting butter that's healthier, quick to make, and fun to mix with berries, jams, or herbs.

SPECIAL EQUIPMENT BAKING SHEET; FOOD PROCESSOR; PIE PLATE OR LARGE BAKING DISH; NONSTICK LARGE SKILLET OR STOVE TOP GRIDDLE; STAND MIXER

- 8 (1-inch / 2.5-cm) thick slices challah, brioche, or any kind of day-old bread
- 4 large eggs, room temperature
- 1 cup (240 ml) half-and-half (fat-free is fine)
- ¼ teaspoon salt
- 5 tablespoons (70 g) sugar
- 5 teaspoons ground cinnamon
- 1 teaspoon pure vanilla extract
- ½ teaspoon almond extract
- 4 tablespoons (60 g) unsalted butter, divided
- warmed maple syrup
- sliced fresh strawberries or blueberries, optional

PREP

Prick the slices of bread all over with a fork (this will allow some of the egg custard to soak in). Preheat the oven to 350° F (180° C) and have the baking sheet ready on the middle rack.

COOK

To make the custard, process the eggs for 30 seconds in the food processor. Add the half-and-half, salt, sugar, cinnamon, vanilla, and almond extract and process another 30 seconds until very well combined.

Pour the custard into the pie plate. Lay the slices of bread in the custard, spoon some of the custard over the top, and soak for 8 minutes. Turn over the bread slices, spoon the custard over the top, and soak for another 8 minutes.

Melt a tablespoon of butter for each 2 slices of bread in the skillet and fry bread for 3 minutes on medium-low heat then turn and fry the other side for 2–3 minutes, until golden on each side. If you fry the bread a couple of pieces at a time, wipe out the pan and add new butter for each batch.

Place all of the slices in the oven on the baking sheet and bake for 5 minutes. Serve immediately with the orange butter and some maple syrup. Seasonal fresh berries scattered on top makes a colorful and healthy addition.

continued >

HOMEMADE ORANGE BUTTER

1 cup (240 ml) heavy cream
(organic, if possible)

2 tablespoons thick-cut orange
marmalade

¼ teaspoon vanilla extract

COOK

Pour the cream into the stand mixer and whip on high. When the cream begins to thicken, after about 5 minutes, scrape down the bowl, continue to whip, and drape a towel over the bowl because the butter will suddenly separate from its liquid, which could splash up. The entire process should take about 13 minutes to form solid butter.

Drain off the liquid and scoop the butter into a sieve to drain. Transfer the butter to the food processor, add the marmalade and vanilla, pulse a few times, then process for about 2 minutes, or until fluffy. Transfer to a serving bowl and serve beside the pain perdu.

IDEAS AND SUBSTITUTIONS

If you have a butter or candy mold, this is when you can have fun with it by pressing your freshly homemade butter into the mold and chilling in the fridge to firm up into shapes before serving.

WICKED CHOCOLATE OMELET FLAMED WITH RUM

Omelette Diabolique au Chocolat, Flambée au Rhum SERVES 2

So very retro when flambéing, this chocolate omelet can light up a significant other's eyes on any day you want to rekindle romance for a chic brunch chez vous *for two.*

SPECIAL EQUIPMENT MEDIUM NONSTICK SKILLET OR OMELET PAN; HEAT-PROOF SERVING PLATE; SMALL SAUCEPAN

- 2 ounces (60 g) semisweet chocolate
- 6 eggs, room temperature, beaten
- ¼ cup (60 ml) heavy cream
- 4 tablespoons (25 g) powdered sugar, plus extra to dust on top
- ¼ teaspoon salt
- 2 tablespoons (30 g) unsalted butter
- ½ shot rum (light, dark, or coconut flavored)

PREP

Place the chocolate in a small stainless steel or glass bowl over a pot of boiling water and melt.

COOK

Whisk together the eggs, cream, melted chocolate, sugar, and salt until well blended. Don't worry if it looks streaky from the melted chocolate. When you cook your omelet those bits and bobs melt into luscious gooey pools.

Melt butter in skillet over low to medium-low heat and pour in the egg mixture. It will look like a lot of eggs for the pan but be patient and gently lift around the edges as it cooks to allow the liquid part of the omelet to get to the bottom of the pan to cook. Keep the top of the omelet a little wetter than normal and when it looks good to you, take a spatula and fold the omelet in half. Slip the omelet onto the serving plate.

Off the heat, pour the rum into the saucepan. Light the rum with a match then pour over the top of the omelet. After the flame has gone out, sprinkle powdered sugar over the top and serve immediately.

IDEAS AND SUBSTITUTIONS

Adding fillings to this omelet can be fun. Think caramelized bananas.

ALSATIAN TWO-CRUSTED MEAT PIE

Tourte Alsacienne aux Deux Viandes SERVES 6–8

Alsatian food is one of my favorite regional foods of France. It tends to be hearty and served in great quantity, and seems to work wonders when it's cold out and you need to eat something substantial. This traditional two-crusted Alsatian tourte *has a combination of ground pork and ground veal and an impressive weight and height, making it perfect for a brunch buffet when friends and family gather.*

SPECIAL EQUIPMENT 10-INCH (25-CM) PIE PLATE; FOOD PROCESSOR; LARGE SOUP POT OR EXTRA-LARGE SKILLET; ROLLING PIN; PASTRY BRUSH; BAKING SHEET

Double Pie Crust

1 cup (2 sticks / 230 g) cold butter

2½ cups (300 g) all-purpose flour, plus more for work surface

½ teaspoon salt

3 teaspoons (15 g) sugar

8 cracks freshly ground black pepper

6 to 8 tablespoons (90 ml to 120 ml) ice water

Filling

2 soft dinner-type rolls

1 cup (240 ml) milk

4 tablespoons (60 g) unsalted butter, divided

1 medium white onion, peeled and finely chopped

1 medium shallot, peeled and finely chopped

1½ pounds (675 g) ground pork loin

½ pound (225 g) ground veal

1 medium russet potato, peeled and finely diced

1 teaspoon salt

10 cracks freshly ground black pepper

½ teaspoon ground cinnamon

½ teaspoon ground cloves

½ cup (120 ml) white wine (like Sylvaner or a dry Riesling)

½ bunch parsley, stems discarded and leaves finely chopped

2 large eggs, beaten

1 egg yolk, beaten with 1 teaspoon water for egg wash

PREP FOR CRUST

Cut butter into cubes and place in the refrigerator for 20 minutes. Butter the pie plate.

COOK

Crust

Place the flour, salt, sugar, and pepper in a food processor and pulse 6 times. Add the butter and pulse 14 times. With the machine running, add water, 1 tablespoon at a time, until the dough begins to come together when pinched.

Transfer dough to a large piece of plastic wrap, fold the wrap over and bring the dough together into a ball. Slice the ball in half. Place each half on a piece of plastic wrap and flatten into a disk. Refrigerate for 30 minutes.

continued >

Filling

Tear apart the rolls and drop them into a bowl with the milk. Push down and allow them to absorb the milk for 15 minutes. Squeeze the rolls of any liquid and finely chop them. Discard any remaining milk.

Meanwhile, cook the onion and shallot in 3 tablespoons (45 g) butter for 4 minutes in a large soup pot over medium heat. Add remaining butter then add the chopped rolls, pork, veal, potato, salt, pepper, cinnamon, and cloves and stir frequently while cooking for 8 minutes. Pour in wine, stir well, and then cool to room temperature.

Transfer to a large bowl. Stir in the parsley and the eggs and mix very well. Pour the contents into a strainer and allow to sit for 5 minutes to drain off any excess liquid then pat with paper towels to completely dry.

Preheat oven to 350° F (180° C).

Roll out one disk of dough on a lightly floured clean work surface. Fit it into the bottom of the pie plate with some overhang. Spoon in the filling, flatten with a spatula, and pat dry again, if needed. Roll out the second disk of dough and place over the top of the pie.

Using your fingers, press down firmly all the way around the edge of the pie to seal. Turn over the overhang all the way around to form a cord then crimp all the way around in a decorative way. Slice 2 slits in the center to vent steam, brush on the egg wash, place the pie on the baking sheet, and bake for 55 minutes. Allow the pie to rest and cool for at least 20 minutes before slicing. Serve with a Riesling wine and a simple tossed salad.

IDEAS AND SUBSTITUTIONS

You can add ½ cup (50 g) finely chopped mushrooms, and use heavy cream instead of milk.

IRRESISTIBLE POTATO, CHEESE, AND CREAM CASSEROLE

Gratin Savoyard aux Pommes de Terre SERVES 6–8

Because Gratin Dauphinois *is made with no cheese, I prefer the potato casserole made in the French Savoie Alps called* Gratin Savoyard *that is made with cheese, eggs, and garlic. Generous amounts of coarsely ground black pepper and freshly grated nutmeg uplift this dish to a serious contender for the best comfort food ever.*

SPECIAL EQUIPMENT 9 X 12-INCH (23 X 30-CM) BAKING DISH; MANDOLIN; LARGE, WIDE SAUCEPAN

2 large cloves garlic

1 tablespoon (15 g) butter, softened

2½ pounds (1.2 kg) Yukon gold potatoes

2 sprigs fresh thyme

3 cups (720 ml) heavy cream

freshly grated nutmeg, to taste

sea salt or kosher salt, to taste

coarsely ground black pepper, to taste

2 large eggs, room temperature, beaten

8 ounces (225 g) Gruyère cheese, grated on the large grate of a box grater

PREP

Preheat the oven to 350° F (180° C).

Slice one of the cloves of garlic in half and rub the halves all over the inside of the baking dish. Peel and mince the remaining clove. After rubbing with garlic, liberally grease the baking dish with the butter.

Peel the potatoes into as perfect ovals as you can. Thinly slice the potatoes on the mandolin or, if using a knife, to the thickness of a coin.

Take the leaves off the thyme sprigs and discard the stems.

COOK

Place the cream, minced garlic, nutmeg, and thyme into the saucepan. Pat the potatoes dry with paper towels and add them to the saucepan. Bring to a boil then remove from heat, cover, and let sit for 15 minutes. Strain the cream into a bowl or large measuring cup.

Transfer half of the potatoes to the baking dish, slightly overlapping them. Sprinkle with salt, lots of pepper, and nutmeg.

Whisk the eggs into the cream then pour half over the potatoes. Scatter half the cheese over the top. Push down the potato slices to submerge them as much as possible in the cream. Add the remaining potatoes, salt, pepper, nutmeg, cream, and cheese.

Bake for 35–40 minutes. Place under the broiler until the top is golden brown. Remove from the broiler and allow to rest for 10 minutes before serving.

IDEAS AND SUBSTITUTIONS

You can make this with zucchini instead of potatoes, or add mushrooms, smoked bacon, or onions, use fat-free half-and-half instead of cream, and if you don't have fresh thyme, use 1 teaspoon dried thyme instead.

TART APPLE TURNOVERS

Chaussons aux Pommes Acidulées MAKES ABOUT 12

Half moon in shape and found in most French bakeries, chaussons aux pommes *(apple slippers) have a smooth, not-too-sweet apple compote filling. Pile these little turnovers high on a plate and serve them with coffee as your brunch guests arrive.*

SPECIAL EQUIPMENT SMALL PLATE, ABOUT 4½ TO 5 INCHES (ABOUT 15 CM) IN DIAMETER; LARGE SKILLET; PASTRY BRUSH; 1 OR 2 BAKING SHEETS LINED WITH PARCHMENT PAPER

1 package frozen puff pastry

4 tablespoons (50 g) sugar, plus sugar for garnishing

¼ teaspoon ground cinnamon

¼ teaspoon ground nutmeg

6 Granny Smith apples

1 organic lemon, zested and juiced

1 egg, room temperature

1 teaspoon water

7 tablespoons (100 g) unsalted butter, divided, with 3 of the tablespoons cut into quarters

¼ teaspoon vanilla extract

PREP

Thaw the puff pastry according to package instructions. Mix together the sugar, cinnamon, and nutmeg.

Peel 5 apples, core, and thinly slice. Place in a bowl and pour most of the lemon juice over them, tossing the apples to coat in the juice. Peel the remaining apple, cut into a small dice, and put in another bowl. Toss in remaining lemon juice.

Beat the egg with the water to make an egg wash.

COOK

Filling

Melt 3 tablespoons (45 g) butter in large skillet, slip in the 5 sliced apples, lemon zest, vanilla, and 2 tablespoons (25 g) of the sugar mixture. Cover and gently cook for about 7 minutes, until apples are tender. Remove the cover, add 1 tablespoon (15 g) of butter, and mash until you have a soft compote of apples. Cool.

Pastry

Roll out the puff pastry to about ¼ inch (6 mm) thick. Use the small plate and knife to cut out approximately 12 circles about 4½–5 (about 15 cm)

inches in diameter then brush the perimeters of the circles with the egg wash. Place 1 tablespoon of the apple compote on half of each circle, and then top with some of the uncooked diced apple. Dot each with one of the quarters of butter and equally divide the remaining cinnamon sugar mixture on top. Fold over the dough of each circle to form a semicircle, pressing down on the edges with your fingers to seal. Roll over the edges into a cord, and pierce each turnover a couple of times with the tip of a knife.

Brush the egg wash all over each turnover, sprinkle with lots of sugar, place them on the baking sheet, and put in the refrigerator for 1 hour.

Preheat oven to 450° F (230° C) then bake for about 19–20 minutes, until golden brown. Cool before serving.

IDEAS AND SUGGESTIONS

The addition of nuts, chocolate chips, dried cranberries, pears, or honey would be delicious. If you have large crystallized baking sugar, sprinkling some on each turnover before baking will yield a lovely crunch on the exterior.

FRENCH ROLLED OMELET WITH CHERRY TOMATOES AND PARMESAN

Omelette Roulée aux Tomates Cerises et au Parmesan SERVES 1

The French have a wonderful way with eggs, either puffing them up into glorious soufflés, rolling them into silky omelets, or poaching or frying them to crown salads or open-face sandwiches.

When I lived in Paris, my lunch was often a simple omelet filled with chopped herbs, omelette aux fines herbes, *French fries, and a glass of wine. The way they make an omelet is to add whatever ingredients they want to the center, then fold the omelet over from both sides and tip it out onto a plate to form a long roll. In my version, I add mayonnaise to the egg mixture, which is not the way it is done in France, but I love the texture and taste it adds (after all, mayonnaise is made from eggs and olive oil, so it isn't as farfetched as it seems)!*

For the perfect omelet, the key is to use the very best quality eggs you can find—free range and organic, if possible.

SPECIAL EQUIPMENT 7- OR 8-INCH (18- OR 20-CM) NONSTICK SKILLET OR OMELET PAN

3 large eggs, room temperature

½ tablespoon mayonnaise

4 cracks coarsely ground black pepper

¼ teaspoon salt

1 tablespoon (15 ml) extra virgin olive oil

¼ cup (25 g) freshly grated Parmesan cheese

8 cherry tomatoes, sliced in half

PREP

Vigorously beat the eggs with the mayonnaise, pepper, and salt.

COOK

Heat the oil in the skillet, pour in the egg mixture, and stir in the center of the pan for a few seconds as you would making scrambled eggs. Then begin to lift the outside edges of the omelet with your spatula while tipping the pan to let any liquid on the top of the omelet slide under and cook. Repeat this all the way around the outer edges until the top of the omelet is set but not dry.

Sprinkle the Parmesan over the omelet, line the tomatoes down the center, then take your spatula and fold over one side, half way, onto the filling. Press down gently with the spatula. Fold over the other side to overlap. Then slip the omelet to the edge of the pan and tip it onto a plate, ending up with the seam side of the omelet facing the bottom of the plate.

IDEAS AND SUBSTITUTIONS

The addition of freshly chopped basil goes well with the cherry tomatoes.

NIÇOISE ONION, BLACK OLIVE, AND ANCHOVY QUICHE

Quiche, Façon Pissaladière SERVES 6

With its buttery, flaky crust and a rich blend of onions, olives, and anchovies, this quiche is my way of making Pissaladière Niçoise, *a form of pizza, into a brunch-inspired dish. Serve with salad and jazz.*

SPECIAL EQUIPMENT 11-INCH (28-CM) QUICHE PAN OR TART TIN WITH REMOVABLE BOTTOM; FOOD PROCESSOR; ROLLING PIN; PARCHMENT PAPER; BAKING BEANS OR RICE TO USE AS WEIGHTS; LARGE SKILLET; KITCHEN SHEARS; BAKING SHEET

Crust

8 tablespoons (1 stick / 120 g) unsalted butter

olive oil

1½ cups (180 g) all-purpose flour

1 teaspoon salt

½ tablespoon sugar

1 large egg yolk

5 tablespoons (75 ml) ice water

Filling

3 tablespoons (45 ml) extra virgin olive oil

2 medium yellow onions, very thinly sliced

3 cloves garlic, peeled and minced

2 teaspoons sugar

6 large eggs, room temperature

2 cups (480 ml) half-and-half for a deep quiche pan, 1½ cups (360 ml) for a shallow one

1 tablespoon herbs de Provence

½ teaspoon salt

8 cracks freshly ground black pepper

20 good-quality canned black olives or oil-cured black olives, pitted and sliced

1 (2-ounce / 60-g) can anchovies in oil, drained

PREP FOR CRUST

Slice the butter into cubes and put in refrigerator until ready to use. Grease the quiche pan with olive oil.

COOK

Crust

Put the flour, salt, and sugar into a food processor. Pulse 4 times. Add butter and process for 10 seconds. Add egg yolk, and with the machine running, pour in water and process until dough comes together in a ball. Transfer the ball to plastic wrap.

Knead a couple of times then press down into a disk and place in the refrigerator to chill for 1 hour.

Roll out dough on a lightly floured work surface with short strokes from the center outwards, turning 45 degrees with each turn, until the dough is large enough to fit into the pan. Lay the dough in the pan, gently press in around the inside corners, and slice off excess dough while allowing a little extra to turn over into a cord and pinch to decorate.

Prick the bottom of the dough several times with a fork and refrigerate for at least 20 minutes while preheating the oven and making the filling.

Preheat the oven to 400° F (200° C)

When the oven is ready, line the dough with parchment paper and baking beans, and bake for 12 minutes. Remove from oven, remove the paper and weights, and put the crust back into the oven to bake for 6–8 minutes, until golden. Remove and cool to room temperature.

Filling

Heat olive oil in the skillet, add the onions and garlic, and cook on medium heat, stirring frequently, until the onions are very soft and golden, about 20 minutes. You may have to do this in 2 skillets at once if all the onions don't fit. Turn up the heat to high, add the sugar, and cook for a couple of minutes, stirring 2–3 times, until the onions caramelize and turn golden.

In a bowl, beat the eggs and whisk in half-and-half, herbs de Provence, salt, and pepper. Scatter the onion mixture and olives evenly over the bottom of the cooled crust.

With kitchen shears, slice half, or more to taste, of the anchovy fillets into $\frac{1}{2}$-inch (1.5 cm) pieces and distribute over the olives. Pour in the egg mixture to fill the quiche.

Place baking sheet on the bottom rack of the oven to catch any possible overflow, and place the quiche on the middle rack. Bake for 30 minutes until set, puffed, and just turning golden. Let the quiche rest for 10 minutes before slicing and serving.

IDEAS AND SUBSTITUTIONS

You can speed up the process by using a good-quality premade crust, but it won't taste as good as one you make, and whipping this one up in a food processor is a breeze.

EGGS POACHED IN BURGUNDY WINE ON GARLIC CROUTONS

Les Œufs en Meurette SERVES 4

One night in Burgundy, I was visiting an old friend and standing in her kitchen. We hadn't planned to be home for dinner, but circumstances had suddenly changed, and we were looking at each other wondering what to do. She opened her refrigerator and stared inside for a minute or two. Then she smiled and handed me an apron.

Soon I learned how to cut thick slices of country bread into big crustless squares which she basted with olive oil and barely fried into warm crisp croutons then placed in the oven to keep warm. It took only minutes before she poached eggs in a wine gravy, placed the eggs on the warmed croutons in our soup bowls, ladled the ruby-colored sauce over them, and scattered crisp bacon all over the top. I was so hungry by then, and so enticed by the aroma in her kitchen, and then so enamored with the taste of this very delicious and satisfying dish, that I asked her for the recipe to take home with me.

It was a lesson about what you can do with what you have on hand, including her use of bouillon cubes, which I have since adopted as my method as well for punching up the flavor in a dish.

SPECIAL EQUIPMENT PASTRY BRUSH; LARGE NONSTICK SKILLET; 4 SHALLOW SOUP BOWLS

- 2 tablespoons (30 g) unsalted butter, room temperature
- 2 tablespoons (15 g) all-purpose flour
- 4 (½-inch / 1.5-cm) slices bread, crusts removed
- 2 tablespoons (30 ml) extra virgin olive oil, plus enough for bread slices

- 8 slices bacon, sliced into small matchsticks
- 2 medium shallots, peeled and finely chopped
- 4 large cloves garlic, peeled and minced
- 4 cups (1 l) red Burgundy wine
- 2 beef bouillon cubes, crushed

- ¼ teaspoon ground cinnamon
- ½ teaspoon sugar
- ¼ teaspoon salt
- 4 cracks freshly ground black pepper
- 8 large eggs, room temperature

PREP

Mash butter and flour together with the back of a spoon in a small bowl to mix well. Preheat oven to 200° F (95° C).

COOK

With the pastry brush, coat the slices of bread with olive oil and fry in the skillet over medium heat just until they begin to look golden, yet are still soft enough to slice with a fork and knife. Keep warm in the oven.

In the same skillet, cook the bacon until crisp. Remove to a plate lined with paper towels. Discard the bacon fat, wipe out the skillet, and add olive oil. Sauté the shallots and garlic over medium heat for 3 minutes. Add wine, bouillon cubes, cinnamon,

sugar, salt, and pepper and simmer for 2 minutes. Whisk in the butter mixture and continue whisking until the sauce thickens.

Crack eggs, one at a time, in a small dish and gently pour each egg into the barely simmering liquid. Poach until whites are firm, about 3–4 minutes.

Place 1 slice of bread in each bowl and scatter crisp bacon all around it. Gently remove the eggs from the sauce with a slotted spoon, place 2 eggs on top of each slice of bread, and then ladle the sauce over the eggs. Serve immediately.

IDEAS AND SUBSTITUTIONS

Pearl onions and button mushrooms are a traditional addition to this dish that comes from the Burgundy region of France.

SOFTLY SCRAMBLED EGGS WITH PEPPERS AND TOMATOES

La Piperade Basquaise SERVES 4

From the southwest of France, piperade *is a classic Basque country dish that you can easily stretch for a late morning crowd. The slow cooking of the vegetables brings out their sweetness, and the last minute addition of cherry tomatoes ensures a little juiciness in every bite.*

Piment d'Espelette, the smoky dried paprika from the village of Espelette in the Basque region, is an authentic and superb addition to the preparation of this dish.

SPECIAL EQUIPMENT LARGE SKILLET

1 sprig fresh thyme or $\frac{1}{2}$ teaspoon dried thyme

2 tablespoons (30 ml) extra virgin olive oil

1 large red bell pepper, thinly sliced

1 large green bell pepper, thinly sliced

1 large onion, peeled and thinly sliced

1 large clove garlic, peeled and minced

$\frac{1}{2}$ teaspoon salt

10 cracks freshly ground black pepper

pinch of piment d'Espelette or dash cayenne

20 cherry tomatoes, sliced in half

8 large eggs, room temperature

2 tablespoons (30 ml) mayonnaise

8 slices warmed baguette

PREP

Pull leaves off the thyme stems. Discard the stems.

COOK

Heat the oil in the skillet on medium heat and add the bell peppers, onion, garlic, salt, pepper, and piment d'Espelette. Stir and cook until tender, about 17 minutes, until it becomes a thick and almost dry mixture. Turn down heat to low, add the thyme and tomatoes, and cook for 2 minutes.

Beat the eggs with the mayonnaise until well blended, and pour into the skillet. Continuously stir on low heat, for about 4–6 minutes, until it turns to softly scrambled eggs. Serve with 2 slices of warmed baguette on each plate.

IDEAS AND SUBSTITUTIONS

The whole idea of piperade is to use peppers, but I find almost any vegetable works well. It's also traditional to add bits of ham to the dish.

BISTRO SALAD WITH POACHED EGG AND BACON

La Salade Lyonnaise aux Lardons SERVES 4

Frisée, or curly endive, is the classic green used in this salad from Lyon. Although most recipes call for the greens to be tossed in a warm dressing, my memories are of a cool salad with a warm egg yolk running in rivulets, mingling with the salad dressing and tempting my piece of bread to sweep in and scoop up the golden liquid.

SPECIAL EQUIPMENT LARGE SKILLET; 4 SERVING PLATES

- 4 small heads of frisée (or enough for 4 servings)
- 4 sprigs fresh tarragon
- 8 slices bacon, sliced into matchsticks
- 1/4 cup (60 ml) white wine or tarragon vinegar, plus 1 teaspoon

- 1/4 teaspoon sea salt, plus a pinch
- 1/2 tablespoon Dijon mustard
- 4 tablespoons (60 ml) extra virgin olive oil
- 1 large clove garlic, peeled and minced
- 1 large shallot, peeled and minced

- 6 cracks coarsely ground black pepper
- 4 large eggs, room temperature
- 4 slices warmed crusty country or sourdough bread
- sea salt flakes, optional

PREP

Slice the bottom off the frisée heads. Wash and spin dry the lettuce then tear into bite-size pieces. Take the leaves off the tarragon sprigs and coarsely chop. Discard the stems.

COOK

Fry the bacon in the skillet until crispy. Drain on paper towels.

Pour 1/4 cup (60 ml) vinegar into a small bowl and whisk in 1/4 teaspoon salt until it is dissolved. Whisk in the mustard until well blended and smooth. Finally, whisk in the olive oil, a little at a time, until smooth. Stir in the garlic, shallot, tarragon, and pepper.

In a large salad bowl, toss the frisée with enough of the dressing to just coat. Evenly divide the salad between the plates, forming nests for an egg to rest on.

Fill the skillet two-thirds full with water and add remaining vinegar and pinch of salt. Bring barely to a simmer with only bubbles on the bottom of the pan. Break the eggs into the pan and poach until they still are soft in the middle, about 3 minutes, basting them several times with spoonfuls of hot water over the top.

Remove the eggs with a slotted spoon and place one on top of each plate of greens. Sprinkle with the crispy bacon and serve immediately with bread. This salad is especially good with a light sprinkle of crunchy salt flakes on the top of the poached egg, a few generous final turns of coarsely ground black pepper, and a glass of chilled white wine.

IDEAS AND SUBSTITUTIONS

The way you wash and dry lettuce can make the difference between a wilted salad and one that is light, with each leaf able to stand on its own. A salad spinner is the key to drying lettuce that will float like feathers into the salad bowl and be dry enough to be able to be coated in every nook and cranny with dressing.

Arugula or escarole can be substituted for the frisée.

CRISPY CINNAMON WALNUT CHOCOLATE PALMIERS

Palmiers à la Cannelle, aux Noix et au Chocolat MAKES 40

Palmiers, *those crispy little elephant ear-shaped pastries that I will drive miles to track down, are actually pretty easy to make at home. Mine are made with chocolate, walnuts, and coated in cinnamon and sugar. Don't worry if you don't use them all up on the day you bake them, as they are even better the next day.*

SPECIAL EQUIPMENT FOOD PROCESSOR; PARCHMENT PAPER; ROLLING PIN; 2 BAKING SHEETS LINED WITH PARCHMENT PAPER

6 ounces (170 g) walnuts

½ cup (80 g) semisweet chocolate chips

¾ cup (150 g) sugar, divided

1 teaspoon vanilla extract

½ teaspoon almond extract

½ tablespoon ground cinnamon

2 sheets frozen puff pastry, thawed

PREP

In the food processor, process the walnuts, chocolate chips, ¼ cup (50 g) sugar, vanilla, and almond extract until well ground. Mix remaining sugar with cinnamon to make cinnamon sugar.

COOK

Lay out a piece of parchment paper that is 20 inches (50 cm) long on your counter. Pour a veil of half of the cinnamon sugar over the sheet in a rectangular area 12 inches (30 cm) long. Lay one sheet puff pastry over the cinnamon sugar and, using the rolling pin, roll it to 12 inches (30 cm) long. The cinnamon sugar will be pressed into the underside of the pastry.

Evenly spread half of the walnut mixture over the surface, pressing down gently to press it into the pastry. Imagine a line half way up the rectangle and begin to tightly roll the pastry from the bottom up to the halfway point. Turn 90 degrees and begin to tightly roll the pastry from the other end towards the halfway point. They are now meeting in the center. Press them together gently, cover with foil or plastic wrap, and refrigerate 45 minutes. Repeat with the second sheet of puff pastry.

Preheat the oven to 425° F (220 °C) 20 minutes before you want to bake the palmiers.

Unwrap one roll at a time and slice in ½-inch (1.5-cm) pieces. Lay each piece on a prepared baking sheet, leaving room in between them so they can spread as they bake. Repeat with the second roll on the second baking sheet.

Bake both sheets for 7–10 minutes, or until the bottoms are golden. Flip the palmiers and bake for another 3 minutes, until golden on top. Remove from oven and cool.

IDEAS AND SUBSTITUTIONS

After you slice the palmiers, try turning them over in more cinnamon sugar for added crispness. If you refrigerate them and bake them the next day, the baking time will be a bit longer, so watch them through the oven window.

CRUSTY BAGUETTE WITH MELTED CHOCOLATE

Pain et Chocolat SERVES 4

Pain et Chocolat is an afternoon snack for school children in France that I like to serve for breakfast or brunch. It couldn't be simpler to make and is a quick substitute for a pain au chocolat, *the chocolate-filled croissants. I almost like these better. Confession—when I really need a happy fix, I make one for myself with a mug of hot chocolate.*

SPECIAL EQUIPMENT TOASTER OVEN OR OVEN

1 medium-size baguette	**1 (4-ounce / 110 g) bar best-quality chocolate (milk or semisweet)**

PREP

Slice the baguette into 4 equal pieces and slice each piece in half lengthwise. Preheat oven to 350° F (180° C).

COOK

Slice the chocolate bars to fit onto the bottom halves of 4 baguette pieces. Place the baguette pieces in the toaster oven to cook until the chocolate is completely melted. Take them out, spread the chocolate with a knife, top with the other pieces of baguette and serve. You can also serve them as is, and toast the other baguette pieces and serve them with butter.

IDEAS AND SUBSTITUTIONS

Use two bars of chocolate if you love chocolate. This is when too much can be a good thing!

FRENCH PRESS COFFEE WITH CALVADOS SHOOTERS

Café Arrosé au Calvados SERVES 2

Making coffee in a French press coffee pot produces a rich, full-bodied brew that you can deliver to the table in style. Buy freshly roasted coffee beans from a local gourmet coffee shop and have them coarsely grind the beans for you. Freshly ground coffee beans, as opposed to preground packages of coffee, make far better coffee in terms of flavor and aroma.

Serve with a shot of Calvados apple brandy like they do in bars and cafés all over France. In Normandy, where it is called café-calva, *they drink all but an inch of their coffee then pour the Calvados into the cup, and bottoms up. I like to drink half the cup, pour in a little Calvados, add a cube of sugar, stir, and sip.*

SPECIAL EQUIPMENT 4-CUP (1-L) FRENCH PRESS COFFEE POT

4 to 6 tablespoons (25 to 35 g) coarsely ground French or espresso coffee

4 cups (1 l) water

2 shots Calvados or apple brandy

PREP

Fill the coffee pot with boiling water and let sit for 1 minute to preheat.

COOK

Pour out and discard the water.

Spoon the coffee in the coffee pot. One tablespoon per cup will make regular strength coffee, and 6 tablespoons will make strong coffee.

Boil water then wait 30 seconds before pouring it into the French press—the reason being that boiling water tends to scald coffee and alter the flavor. Put the lid on the French press and let sit for 4 minutes before pressing down on the filter until it can go no further.

Pour the coffee into cups and serve with a shot of Calvados. You'll have enough for 2 cups each.

IDEAS AND SUBSTITUTIONS

Chocolates on the side wouldn't hurt!

To make a *café au lait,* heat some milk just to the boiling point and pour it halfway up your coffee cup, filling the rest with coffee.

CHAMPAGNE WITH BLACK CURRANT LIQUEUR

Kir Royal MAKES 4

Kir Royal is an elegant drink made with Champagne and a touch of black current liqueur, crème de cassis. A great brunch starter, this blushing bubbly is a light apéritif *that offers a welcome change from orangey mimosas.*

Kir refers to the original drink named after a priest, Canon Félix Kir, who was mayor of Dijon for 23 years and who served a white wine and cassis blend at official functions. It was soon adopted by restaurants in the area and became popular throughout France. Kir Royal, made with Champagne rather than white wine, is its sophisticated cousin.

SPECIAL EQUIPMENT 4 CHAMPAGNE FLUTES

1 bottle dry French Brut Champagne or dry sparkling wine

4 teaspoons (20 ml) crème de cassis

PREP

Chill the Champagne glasses. Chill the Champagne.

COOK

Add 1 teaspoon (5 ml) crème de cassis to each glass then fill with Champagne.

IDEAS AND SUGGESTIONS

These are delicious with a couple of fresh raspberries or blackberries tossed in.

THICK HOT CHOCOLATE

Le Chocolat Chaud SERVES 4

I remember the first time I had hot chocolate in France. Snow was beginning to fall. The hot chocolate was served in a bowl that you picked up with both hands and drank from, making you feel like a child again. Pleasure poured down my throat and warmed every inch of me.

Chocolat Chaud is often a touch thicker than we are used to. Try this recipe, and see if you don't hear Edith Piaf singing La Vie En Rose*! You'll never use powdered mixes again.*

SPECIAL EQUIPMENT MEDIUM SAUCEPAN

4 cups (1 l) milk, divided

4 ounces (110 g) best-quality bittersweet chocolate, finely chopped

4 ounces (110 g) best-quality semisweet chocolate, finely chopped

pinch of ground cinnamon

1 tablespoon (8 g) cornstarch

COOK

In the saucepan, heat 3½ cups (850 ml) of the milk until it just comes to a boil. Remove from the heat and whisk in the chocolate and cinnamon.

With a fork, mix the cornstarch with the remaining milk, add to the saucepan, whisk, and bring back to a boil while continuously whisking. When the hot chocolate has thickened, pour and serve.

IDEAS AND SUBSTITUTIONS

Make it crazy good with a dollop of whipped cream on top. If you like your hot chocolate sweeter, substitute milk chocolate. Also a little grated orange zest on top adds an intriguing aroma and flavor. And for adult hot chocolate, you can start with a little brandy at the bottom of each cup.

SOUPS, SANDWICHES, AND SIMPLE PLEASURES

The long, lingering multiple-course meals the French are well-known for are still taken at home or in restaurants, while at the same time, street food and portable meals on the run when there is no time for sitting down are on the increase. Sandwiches are the preferred fast comfort food, normally made on a baguette. The Parisian *jambon beurre*, which is simply made with sweet butter and ham, is the most popular.

Soups, as well, can be a comfort on their own. Although a traditional first course before a meal, soup is casual and substantial enough to be enjoyed with a slice of good bread.

And then there are the simple pleasures, the ones you reach for that are just for the sake of eating . . . and don't have to be part of a meal.

FRENCH ONION SOUP GRATINÉE

Soupe Gratinée à l'Oignon SERVES 4

The story goes that late one night, faced with a very hungry King Louis XIV, the palace chef improvised with what was on hand and created an onion soup. Its ingredients were onions cooked in butter, with Champagne added to make the broth.*

French Onion Soup Gratinée was made famous in the nineteenth century by workers at the Parisian market Les Halles. They ordered it as a meal in the early hours of the morning after working all night. Au Pied de Cochon, a restaurant in the area where Les Halles used to be, was and still is, known for its onion soup gratinée, and that is where my first memory of French onion soup comes from.

A crust of bread, some onions, a bit of cheese, and you have one of the most satisfying and filling soups possible in your own home. I may, someday, try making it with Champagne for a hint of what it must have tasted like the night it was invented.

SPECIAL EQUIPMENT LARGE SAUCEPAN OR SOUP POT; BAKING SHEET COVERED WITH ALUMINUM FOIL; 4 SOUP BOWLS

4 large onions

3 tablespoons (45 g) unsalted butter, softened, divided

2 tablespoons (30 ml) cognac, plus 2 teaspoons

1 teaspoon Dijon mustard

1 teaspoon fresh thyme leaves

4 tablespoons (60 ml) extra virgin olive oil

2 teaspoons sugar

½ tablespoon all-purpose flour

4 cups (1 l) chicken stock

salt and pepper, to taste

8 slices baguette

1 cup (100 g) grated Gruyère cheese

PREP

Slice the onions in half and then half again. Peel and place each on a cutting board, flat side down, and slice into thick ½-inch (1.5-cm) slices.

In a small bowl using a fork, mix 1 tablespoon of the butter with 2 tablespoons cognac, mustard, and thyme leaves.

Preheat the broiler.

COOK

Melt remaining butter into the olive oil in the saucepan. Add the onions. Cook very slowly on medium-low heat until they have a deep brown color, about 17 minutes. Turn the heat up to medium-high, add the sugar, and stir for 1 minute.

Remove from the heat, add the flour, and stir well to cover the onions. Pour in the stock, stir, place back on the heat, and bring to a boil. Turn down to a simmer and cook for 5 minutes. Add salt and pepper.

Whisk in the butter and cognac mixture and bring back to a low simmer until ready to serve.

Meanwhile, place the slices of baguette on the baking sheet. Equally divide the cheese on top of 4 of the slices and place under the broiler until the cheese is just melted and bubbly. Four of the slices will have no cheese.

Place one slice without cheese in the bottom of each bowl. Pour ½ teaspoon cognac on top of each to soak the bread. Ladle the soup into the bowls and top with a slice of baguette with melted cheese. Serve.

IDEAS AND SUGGESTIONS

Use any cheese you may already have on hand. Although Gruyère is the traditional cheese for French onion soup, any cheese that melts well works.

*Dione Lucas, *The Dione Lucas Book of French Cooking* (Boston, Little, Brown and Company, 1947), 160.

PÉRIGORD GARLIC AND CHICKEN SOUP

Tourain du Périgord SERVES 4

Especially warming in cold weather, the garlic soup made in the Périgord region of France is normally started with duck or goose fat in which the onions and garlic are cooked before adding stock and wine. This one is made using butter, and it's a recipe I make into a substantial meal by adding some chicken.

People who live in the Périgord region add a little red wine as they reach the bottom of their bowl of soup. They mix it around with their spoon, lift the bowl, and drink the wine-soup mixture from their bowl. This custom is called faire chabrot. *You will impress the natives if you travel there and do chabrot at the end of your soup!*

SPECIAL EQUIPMENT LARGE SAUCEPAN OR SOUP POT; 4 SOUP BOWLS

2 boneless, skinless chicken thighs

2 large eggs, room temperature

3 tablespoons (45 g) unsalted butter

15 cloves garlic, peeled and finely sliced

1 medium-small onion, peeled and finely sliced

1/4 cup (30 g) all-purpose flour

4 cups (1 l) chicken stock

1 chicken bouillon cube, crushed

1/2 cup (120 ml) dry white wine

1/8 teaspoon herbes de Provence

salt and pepper, to taste

3 teaspoons red wine vinegar

4 thickly sliced country, sourdough, or baguette bread slices to fit in soup bowls

PREP

Poach chicken thighs for about 30 minutes, until done. When cool, shred the meat with a fork and knife. Separate the egg yolks from the whites into 2 small bowls.

COOK

In the saucepan, melt the butter, throw in all of the garlic and onion at once, and cook until just soft. Remove from the heat and stir in the flour to coat the garlic and onion. Add the stock and bouillon cube then stir, return to the heat, and simmer for 15 minutes. Add the wine and herbes de Provence to the soup and simmer for another 5 minutes. Add salt and pepper.

Whisk the egg yolks into the vinegar then whisk into the soup and cook until thickened, about 2 minutes. Add the egg whites and, with a fork, continuously swirl the egg whites into the soup until you see them form white threads.

To serve, place a slice of bread in each bowl. Evenly divide the chicken on top of the bread and ladle the soup on top.

IDEAS AND SUGGESTIONS

For a lighter and quicker meal, eliminate the bread and chicken and the soup will still be loaded with flavor and texture.

CREAMIEST POTATO AND LEEK SOUP WITH CHOPPED SCALLIONS AND CRUMBLED BACON

Vichyssoise, Cébettes et Poitrine Fumée SERVES 4–6

French Chef Louis Diat, of the New York Ritz-Carlton, created and named the soup called Vichyssoise *decades ago in honor of one his mother used to make in France. Chef Diat's recipe uses cream and chives and is served cold. I like to make it the way his mother did, with milk and served hot. The addition of freshly chopped scallions and crumbled bacon is my contribution to their creations.**

SPECIAL EQUIPMENT LARGE SOUP POT; BLENDER OR STICK IMMERSION BLENDER

- 2 medium leeks
- 4 tablespoons (60 g) unsalted butter
- 2 medium shallots, peeled and finely chopped
- 4 cloves garlic, peeled and finely chopped
- 4 cups (1 l) chicken or vegetable stock
- 1 pound (450 g) Yukon gold potatoes, unpeeled, cleaned, and diced
- 1 cup (240 ml) milk, plus more to thin, if desired
- ¼ teaspoon salt
- 1 crack freshly ground black pepper
- 4 scallions, sliced into very thin rounds
- 4 slices bacon, cooked and crumbled

PREP

To trim the leeks, slice off the root end. Pull off the tough exterior leaves and slice off the top, leaving 3 inches (8 cm) of the green part so that you have the white and light-green interiors of the leeks. Slice leeks in half vertically, wash under running water, dry, and slice into ¼-inch (6-mm) pieces. You should have about 3 cups.

COOK

In the soup pot, melt the butter then add the leeks, shallots, and garlic. Cover and cook on medium-low heat until limp, about 8–10 minutes. Pour in the stock and potatoes and cook until fork tender, about 30 minutes. Remove from the heat and cool for 15 minutes.

Purée the mixture in batches in a blender, or blend with a stick immersion blender, until it is smooth then add it back to the soup pot and heat. Whisk in the milk, and add salt and pepper. Add a little more milk if you would like a thinner consistency. Ladle into bowls and heap the chopped scallions and crumbled bacon into the center of each bowl.

IDEAS AND SUGGESTIONS

To make Chef Louis Diat's soup, vichyssoise, simply serve this soup cold, adding some cream and chives. I like to make vichyssoise in the summer and garnish it with a dollop of savory whipped cream flavored with salt, chives, and a touch of horseradish—or finely chopped smoked salmon to dress it up.

*Marian Morash, *The Victory Garden Cookbook* (Alfred A. Knopf, 1982), 159

ROASTED BUTTERNUT SQUASH SOUP WITH CANDIED CHESTNUTS

Soupe de Courge Musquée Rôtie et Marrons Glacés SERVES 6

Deriving its flavor from the caramelized roasted vegetables, this is a light satisfying soup made more interesting with chestnuts candied with vanilla, soft and sweet, mounded in the center of each bowl.

SPECIAL EQUIPMENT BAKING PAN WITH SIDES; FOOD PROCESSOR; SOUP POT; SAUCEPAN; PARCHMENT PAPER

1 large butternut squash or 2½ pounds (1.2 kg) precut butternut squash cubes

1 medium white onion, peeled and sliced into eighths

1 medium carrot, sliced into 1-inch (2.5-cm) pieces

3 tablespoons (45 ml) extra virgin olive oil, divided

2 tablespoons (25 g) sugar, plus ¾ cup (150 g)

½ teaspoon salt

4 cups (1 l) vegetable broth

½ cup (120 ml) water

½ teaspoon vanilla extract

2 cups (375 g) bottled chestnuts, sliced in half

PREP

Grease baking pan with olive oil. If using a whole squash, slice in half, seed, then slice into 1-inch (2.5-cm) chunks and peel.

Preheat the oven to 400° F (200° C).

COOK

In the baking pan, toss the squash, onion, and carrot with 2 tablespoons (30 ml) olive oil, 2 tablespoons (25 g) sugar, and salt and roast about 45 minutes until they are caramelized and tender. Cool to room temperature.

Scrape everything from the baking pan into a food processor in batches and purée, incorporating 1 cup (240 ml) of broth in each batch. With the last batch, add remaining olive oil when you purée it. Transfer all of the purée to the soup pot and heat.

Bring the water to a boil in the saucepan, add the remaining sugar and vanilla, and stir on medium-high heat until it turns thick, about 4–5 minutes. Add the chestnuts and stir, cooking until most of the moisture evaporates, about 3 minutes. Transfer to a piece of parchment paper, spread out, and break into pieces. Cool.

To serve, ladle hot soup into bowls and spoon the candied chestnuts into the center of each bowl.

IDEAS AND SUBSTITUTIONS

Instead of chestnuts, try halved walnuts and raw diced pears.

TOASTED HAM AND CHEESE SANDWICH WITH FRIED EGG

Croque-Madame MAKES 4 SANDWICHES

Invented in a Paris café in 1910, the croque-monsieur *was originally a melted cheese and ham sandwich sautéed in butter. Eventually other Parisian cafés began serving their own versions to the point where the sandwich evolved to the way it is served today, with a topping of béchamel sauce, grated cheese, then run under the broiler until bubbly and golden. The* croque-madame *is a variation of croque-monsieur which features a fried egg on top.*

Croque means crunch, so it's important for the bread to be crunchy while the inside is oozy with melted cheese.

SPECIAL EQUIPMENT SAUCEPAN; TOASTER; BAKING SHEET; SKILLET

- 4 tablespoons (60 g) unsalted butter
- 4 tablespoons (30 g) all-purpose flour
- 1 cup (240 ml) milk
- 2 teaspoons Dijon mustard
- 2 dashes ground nutmeg
- 8 slices white sandwich bread
- 4 thin slices ham
- 3 cups (300 g) grated Gruyère cheese, divided
- 4 large eggs, room temperature

PREP

Preheat the oven to 450° F (230° C).

COOK

In the saucepan, melt the butter, add the flour, and whisk well. Slowly whisk in milk and cook until thickened. Whisk in mustard and nutmeg. Set aside.

Lightly toast the bread in the toaster. Place 4 slices on the baking sheet. Spread a little sauce on the slices and top with a piece of ham. Place ½ cup (50 g) cheese on each slice of ham then top with the remaining slices of bread.

Evenly divide the rest of the sauce over the top of the sandwiches, add the remaining cheese, and bake for 5 minutes. While the sandwiches are baking, fry the eggs in the skillet.

Turn off the oven and preheat the broiler. Run the sandwiches under the broiler until they are bubbly and slightly browned. Top each with a fried egg and serve hot.

IDEAS AND SUBSTITUTIONS

Side the sandwiches with a simple green salad for a light lunch or dinner. Optional additions to béchamel sauce: finely chopped onion, fresh tarragon, or parsley.

TOASTED HAM, BLUE CHEESE, AND MOZZARELLA SANDWICH WITH MUSTARD CREAM SAUCE

Croque-Monsieur au Bleu à ma Façon SERVES 4

This is my version of a croque-monsieur au bleu *I had one day at a café near the Seine in Paris. It was made on Poilâne sourdough bread with a slab of creamy Bleu d'Auvergne cheese and a thick cut of baked ham. Covered in a béchamel sauce and run under the grill, it was oozy and crispy and warm at the same time.*

Autumn leaves swept by me in a great gust of cold wind that day as I sat at my outdoor table, oblivious to the blackening sky and coming storm because my attention was so thoroughly riveted on this most amazing sandwich.

SPECIAL EQUIPMENT BROILER TRAY; ALUMINUM FOIL; TOASTER; PASTRY BRUSH; NONSTICK SKILLET; BAKING SHEET; SAUCEPAN

- **2 ounces (60 g) blue cheese, chilled**
- **2 ounces (60 g) mozzarella, chilled**
- **½ sweet onion, minced**
- **8 slices sourdough bread**
- **4 thin slices ham**
- **2 teaspoons Dijon mustard**
- **coarsely ground black pepper, to taste**
- **2 tablespoons (30 g) unsalted butter, melted**
- **2 tablespoons (30 ml) extra virgin olive oil**

PREP

Coarsely grate the blue cheese and mozzarella on the big holes of a box grater.

Line the broiler tray with aluminum foil. Preheat the oven to 300° F (150° C).

COOK

Make the sandwiches first, as the sauce should not be made too far ahead. Scoop the blue cheese and mozzarella into a bowl and lightly toss to combine. Take out 4 tablespoons (40 g) and reserve for later. Add the onion and toss again.

Lightly toast bread slices in the toaster. Lay ham slices on 4 slices of bread that have been lightly smeared with mustard. Pack cheese mixture into a ½-cup (120-ml) measuring cup then invert on a slice

of ham and press down with fingers to compress the cheese. Coarsely grind black pepper over the top of the cheese mixture. Repeat this process with remaining slices. Top each with a slice of bread and press down gently to compact again.

Using the pastry brush, paint the top slice of each sandwich with butter. Warm olive oil in the skillet then cook 2 sandwiches at a time on medium-low heat. Press down firmly with a spatula and brown for about 2–3 minutes until the bread is crisp. Flip over the sandwiches, paint the top slice of bread with butter, and brown until bottom slice is crisp and cheese is starting to melt.

Place each sandwich as you make it in the oven on the baking sheet to keep warm. When all 4 sandwiches are in the oven, turn off the heat and preheat the broiler.

Lay the sandwiches on the broiler pan, top each with the Mustard Cream Sauce, and 1 tablespoon of the reserved cheese mixture. Pop under the broiler for 3–5 minutes, until bubbly and golden. Serve immediately with a fork and knife.

MUSTARD CREAM SAUCE

4 tablespoons (60 g) unsalted butter

4 tablespoons (30 g) all-purpose flour

1 cup (240 ml) milk

2 teaspoons Dijon mustard

freshly grated nutmeg, to taste

2 dashes cayenne pepper

¼ teaspoon salt

6 cracks coarsely ground black pepper

COOK

In the saucepan, melt the butter, add the flour, and whisk well. Slowly whisk in milk and cook until thickened and bubbly. Whisk in mustard, nutmeg, cayenne, salt, and pepper. Take a taste and add more mustard, salt, or some pepper, if desired.

IDEAS AND SUBSTITUTIONS

Use any kind of blue cheese—Blue Castello, Bleu d'Auvergne, Roquefort, domestic, or Danish. I almost always add some grated mozzarella to any grilled cheese sandwich I make for melt appeal.

If you have a panini press, you can easily make these then top them with the sauce and run under the broiler.

CHILLED LYONNAISE POTATO AND SAUSAGE SALAD

Salade de Pommes de Terre et Cervelas de Lyon SERVES 4

If you ordered this in a bistro in Lyon, the artisanal sausages would be made with pistachios and the salad would be served warm. I prefer to serve it chilled in the summer, heaped over a handful of dressed greens, with a crisp white wine.

SPECIAL EQUIPMENT 2 SAUCEPANS; 4 SALAD PLATES

3 sprigs fresh tarragon

4 unsmoked pork sausages, pistachio or garlic

2 pounds (900 g) white potatoes, peeled and halved

salt and freshly ground black pepper, to taste

¼ cup (60 ml) dry white wine

2 teaspoons Dijon mustard, plus more to serve with salad

3 tablespoons (45 ml) white wine or tarragon vinegar

½ cup (120 ml) extra virgin olive oil

2 medium shallots, peeled and minced

3 cloves garlic, peeled and minced

4 handfuls mixed salad greens

1 large long baguette, warmed in oven and sliced

PREP

Remove the tarragon leaves from the stems and mince. Discard the stems.

COOK

In one saucepan, cover the sausages with water and cook at a simmer until done, about 35 minutes. When cool to the touch, slice and place into a large bowl.

At the same time in the other saucepan, cover the potatoes with water and cook at a simmer until done, about 20 minutes, or until a fork can easily pierce. Drain in a colander to cool then slice into thick chunks and place into the bowl with the sausages. Salt and pepper then pour the wine over the top and gently mix to coat.

In another bowl, vigorously whisk together the mustard and vinegar. Slowly drip in oil as you

continuously whisk until well blended. Whisk in the shallots, garlic, and tarragon and add salt and pepper. Spoon a little of the dressing over the top of the salad greens and toss to barely coat. Divide the greens between the plates.

Pour the rest of the dressing over the potato and sausage salad and very gently toss with a fork to coat with the dressing. Mound on top of the greens and serve with mustard, a pepper mill, and warm slices of baguette.

IDEAS AND SUBSTITUTIONS

You could also make this with whole fingerling potatoes and not slice them.

SUMMERY SALADE NIÇOISE SANDWICHES

Le Pan Bagnat SERVES 4

Pan Bagnat *is a sandwich invented in Nice in the south of France. It is so popular there that they even bake a special roll for it. The quintessential Riviera beach food, a pan bagnat features super fresh ingredients almost identical to a* salade Niçoise, *which was also invented in Nice.*

The secret is to allow the sandwiches to sit for at least an hour before serving to absorb the vinaigrette and to let the ingredients mingle and get to know each other.

SPECIAL EQUIPMENT PASTRY BRUSH

4 extra-large crusty rolls

4 cups (200 g) loosely packed lettuce

8 large basil leaves

1 cup (240 ml) extra virgin olive oil, plus enough to drizzle on sandwiches

½ teaspoon Dijon mustard

6 tablespoons (90 ml) red wine vinegar, plus enough to drizzle on sandwiches

¼ teaspoon sugar

8 anchovy filets, minced

2 cloves garlic, peeled and minced

8 cracks coarsely ground black pepper

2 (5- to 6-ounce / 140- to 170-g) cans best-quality solid light tuna in olive oil, drained and oil reserved

1 cup (125 g) oil-cured black olives, sliced

2 medium tomatoes, sliced into 8 slices

2 hard-boiled large eggs, peeled and sliced

PREP

Slice the rolls in half horizontally and scoop out a little of the soft interior. Clean and dry lettuce and basil leaves. Tear basil leaves and add to lettuce.

COOK

In a bowl, vigorously whisk together the olive oil, mustard, vinegar, sugar, anchovies, garlic, and pepper. Toss the salad with only enough vinaigrette to barely coat the leaves. Reserve the rest of the vinaigrette.

With the pastry brush, paint the insides of the rolls with the remaining vinaigrette. Lightly mash the tuna with a fork to soften, adding drops of reserved oil, if needed.

Fill each roll with salad, olives, 2 slices tomato, tuna, a little drizzle of olive oil and vinegar, and slices of egg. Put the tops on the sandwiches and press down. Wrap tightly in plastic wrap and refrigerate for at least 1 hour before serving.

IDEAS AND SUBSTITUTIONS

Make these on little slider rolls for appetizers for a party.

BAGUETTE SANDWICH WITH HAM AND SWEET BUTTER

Le Jambon Beurre SERVES 4

One of the first things I do in the morning in Paris is to go out to a café and order a café crème *and a* jambon-beurre *for breakfast. I may grab one to take on a road trip for lunch or for a picnic with friends. It's a fast food favorite in France, afford-able, portable, and sold just about everywhere including cafés, bars, bistros, bakeries, and even in department store food halls.*

What is this popular sandwich made of? Only three ingredients—a baguette, sweet butter, and ham. Find a freshly baked baguette, buy sweet butter from France, if you can find it, and have the deli thinly slice boiled ham. The only change I make is to sprinkle a few crunchy sea salt flakes over the butter for a sandwich that is one of life's simplest pleasures!

1 baguette

4 tablespoons (60 g) unsalted best-quality butter, room temperature

sea salt flakes (like Malden)

4 ounces (110 g) thinly sliced boiled ham, about 8 slices

COOK

Slice the baguette into 4 pieces and slice each lengthwise. Spread 1 tablespoon (15 g) butter on the bottom half of each piece. Sprinkle with a few sea salt flakes. Add two slices of ham on each and top with the remaining slices of bread.

IDEAS AND SUGGESTIONS

Thinly sliced cornichons (gherkins) add a crunchy dimension to this already delicious sandwich.

RUSTIC COUNTRY PÂTÉ WITH GREEN PEPPERCORNS AND PISTACHIOS

Pâté au Poivre Vert aux Pistaches MAKES 1 LOAF

I used to meet my husband after work for picnics when we lived in Paris. Sometimes we'd take the ramp down to the Quais along the Seine and stroll until we found a bench to sit on. The Eiffel Tower would be before us, and we could watch the river boats go by. More often than not, our picnic supper would be sliced pâté, a baguette, some cheese, and a bottle of red wine.

It was peaceful there on the bench and, if we waited long enough, we could see the sky turn pale pink and long pastel ribbons form on the river.

Pâté is a quintessential part of everyday life in France, and every region and household seems to make their own version. In the north of France, in French Flanders, they even put rhubarb in their pâté! This one you serve as a slice on a piece of bread, and it has crunchy green peppercorns and pistachios.

SPECIAL EQUIPMENT MORTAR AND PESTLE; 9 X 5-INCH (23 X 13-CM) LOAF PAN; SMALL SAUCEPAN; ALUMINUM FOIL; LARGE BAKING DISH; INSTANT-READ THERMOMETER; BRICK OR HEAVY OBJECT TO ACT AS A WEIGHT

1 pound (450 g) thinly sliced bacon, divided

6 large cloves garlic

3 shallots

1½ tablespoons (8 g) dried green peppercorns

1 beef bouillon cube or 1 teaspoon beef base

6 tablespoons (90 ml) water

3 tablespoons (45 ml) extra virgin olive oil

3 tablespoons (25 g) all-purpose flour

1½ teaspoons (½ packet) unflavored gelatin

¼ cup (60 ml) heavy cream

½ cup (120 ml) cognac

2 large eggs, room temperature, beaten

1½ teaspoons kosher salt

16 cracks freshly ground black pepper

1 teaspoon freshly ground nutmeg

1 teaspoon ground cloves

1½ pounds (675 g) ground pork

½ pound (225 g) ground beef

½ pound (225 g) diced chicken livers, membranes removed

1 tablespoon fresh thyme leaves

1 cup (120 g) whole unsalted, roasted pistachios, sliced in half

PREP

Finely chop 6 slices of bacon and toss in a large mixing bowl. Peel and mince the garlic and shallots and add to bowl. Crush the green peppercorns in mortar and pestle, or very coarsely chop using a knife.

Heat oven to 350° F (180° C).

COOK

Line the loaf pan with bacon by laying slices horizontally all the way down the pan with ends hanging over to wrap over the top. Use more, cut in half, to line the ends of the pan.

In the small saucepan over medium-low heat, melt the bouillon cube or beef base in the water.

continued >

Turn off the heat. With a fork, beat in the olive oil, flour (1 tablespoon at a time), and gelatin; stir well to mix. Over medium-low heat, slowly add the cream, stir to mix, and heat until it boils, thickens, and is bubbly. Remove from heat and cool to room temperature. Whisk in the cognac, eggs, and spices.

Add the pork, beef, chicken livers, and cream mixture to the bowl and mix well, using your hands like a 5-finger whisk, stirring round and round until the mixture is very well blended. Then mix in the thyme, peppercorns, and pistachios.

Transfer the pâté mixture to the loaf pan, pressing down with your fingers to compress and pack it in tightly. Fold over the bacon to cover the top so that it bastes the pâté as it bakes. Cover with the remaining slices of bacon.

Cover with aluminum foil greased with olive oil and place in the baking dish. Boil water and pour into the dish so that the water comes halfway up the loaf pan. Bake until the instant-read thermometer registers 160° F (71° C), about 2 hours. Check the temperature at 1 hour.

Remove from the oven and cool. Place the brick on the top of the pâté to weigh it down, and place in the refrigerator for 24 hours.

Remove the pâté from the loaf pan and cut into ½-inch (1.5-cm) slices. Serve with mustard, cornichons, and crusty bread.

IDEAS AND SUBSTITUTIONS

For the holidays, use pink and green peppercorns for a festive look. Other additions could include capers, dried chopped apricots, or prunes.

If you don't want to use bacon, you can line the pan with parchment paper. The pâté will keep for one week in the refrigerator.

OLIVE OIL FRENCH FRIES WITH ROSEMARY SALT

Les Pommes Frites, Sel au Romarin SERVES 4

French fries are so important to me that I willingly spend extra to fry them in good-quality olive oil, as opposed to neutral-flavored vegetable oils, because they taste so much better.

Slice the potatoes in the morning, leave them to soak all day in water, and make them in the evening. The soaking removes starch from the outside of the potatoes so they fry up very crispy.

Cooking the French fries proceeds in two steps—a first frying at a lower temperature and a second frying at a higher temperature. This method frees up my time when I am preparing a meal because I can do the first step well ahead of time, then 5 minutes before I need them, I can ease the fries back into hot oil and cook them the final time. Quickly drained on paper towels and sprinkled with rosemary salt, they are ready to serve.

SPECIAL EQUIPMENT HEAVY LARGE POT OR DEEP WIDE SKILLET; CANDY OR FRYING THERMOMETER

4 large russet potatoes   **olive oil for frying**

PREP

In the morning, peel the potatoes. Slice into ¼-inch (6-mm) slices then stack the slices and slice again into thin batons. Place in a large bowl of water and refrigerate until the evening, or for at least 6 hours.

COOK

Take the potatoes out of the water and thoroughly dry them on paper towels.

Fill the pot or skillet with about 2 inches (5 cm) of oil and attach the thermometer. Heat the oil to 300° F (150° C), ease in just enough fries so they can cook in one layer and still be completely covered with oil,

and fry without disturbing (timing will depend on how thickly the fries are sliced). You want to cook them until they are soft and limp, so test with a fork. Remove fries with a slotted spoon to paper towels. Bring the oil back to 300° F (150° C) and repeat this process with the rest of the potatoes. Reserve the oil.

When you are ready to serve the French fries, bring the temperature of the oil to 375° F (190° C). Ease in enough fries to cook in one layer and fry until golden brown, about 2 minutes. Remove to paper towels to drain and repeat process for any remaining fries. Sprinkle with rosemary salt and serve.

ROSEMARY SALT

SPECIAL EQUIPMENT FOOD PROCESSOR; PARCHMENT PAPER

2 sprigs fresh rosemary   **¼ cup (65 g) sea salt or kosher salt**

PREP

Pull off the leaves from the rosemary sprigs. Discard the stems.

COOK

Drop the rosemary leaves and salt into the food processor and pulse until leaves are finely chopped. Spread out on parchment paper until ready to use.

IDEAS AND SUBSTITUTIONS

Add duck fat to your oil for a richer flavor or use all duck fat.

HEAVENLY MASHED POTATOES WITH GARLIC AND MELTED CHEESE

L'Aligot comme en Aubrac SERVES 6

Smooth and rich, sort of like mashed potatoes with lots of cheese in it, aligot *is a sensational way to cook potatoes that sides beautifully with a grilled steak or chicken.*

The dish comes from Aubrac in the south of France and is made with Cantal cheese, which can be hard to find so I use a very sharp white cheddar.

You don't have to wait to go to heaven . . . sometimes you can find it on earth.

SPECIAL EQUIPMENT LARGE SAUCEPAN; SMALL SAUCEPAN; FOOD PROCESSOR

8 russet potatoes (2 pounds / 900 g), peeled and quartered

6 teaspoons (30 g) salt, divided

1 cup (240 ml) heavy cream

½ cup (120 ml) milk

8 tablespoons (1 stick / 120 g) unsalted butter

2 large cloves garlic, peeled and minced

4 cracks freshly ground black pepper, plus more for garnish

8 ounces (225 g) sharp white cheddar or French Cantal cheese, grated

COOK

Place potatoes in the large saucepan and cover with water. Add 3 teaspoons salt, bring to a boil, partially cover, and simmer until the potatoes are tender.

Meanwhile, in the small saucepan, heat the cream, milk, butter, garlic, and remaining salt until it comes to a simmer then take off the heat.

When the potatoes are done, drain them in a colander for 2 minutes. Pour out all of the water from the saucepan and dry. Put the potatoes and milk mixture in the food processor and process for 15 seconds. You may have to do this in 2 batches. Scrape down the sides, add pepper, and process another 15 seconds.

Scoop the potatoes back into the large saucepan and begin to cook on low heat. Add a handful of cheese and stir vigorously with a wooden spoon. Add another handful and stir continuously until incorporated. Continue until you have used all the cheese and the texture is smooth and glossy. The entire process will take anywhere from 8–12 minutes. Serve right away with a final crack of black pepper over the top.

IDEAS AND SUBSTITUTIONS

Using Raclette cheese or adding in some mozzarella will yield greater elasticity to the final product. You can also substitute white wine for the milk, which yields more of a fondue flavor.

FAMILY-STYLE RECIPES

I asked my French friends what would be their go-to recipes to make for their families, and we came up with this list—dishes they make as casseroles or can quickly sauté and serve. And although slow cookers are not widely used in France, they are available in stores there under the name *mijoteuse*. A couple of the working moms I know swear by them for some dishes. So I've included French-style slow-cooker recipes in this chapter in the interest of shortening the time it normally takes to make a couple of labor-intensive authentic French dishes that are French family favorites.

FRENCH MAC 'N' CHEESE

Gratin de Macaronis au Munster SERVES 6-8

Paul Bocuse, one of France's master chefs, is largely responsible for making macaroni and cheese a favorite comfort food in France. His version uses long tubular macaroni noodles baked in a béchamel sauce with cheese grated over the top and a few slivers of truffles slipped in here and there. French families have taken off with it, creating many variations of the dish. Mine is a mild and creamy one, using lots of Munster cheese from northern France, and macaroni that has been cooked in a combination of milk and water.

SPECIAL EQUIPMENT 8- TO 12-CUP (2- TO 3-L) BAKING DISH OR DEEP 2.5-QUART (2.5-L) BAKING DISH; LARGE SAUCEPAN

6 tablespoons (90 g) unsalted butter, plus butter to grease baking dish

4 cups (1 l) milk

3 cups (720 ml) water

1 pound (450 g) macaroni

6 tablespoons (45 g) all-purpose flour

2 cups (480 ml) heavy cream or half-and-half

1 chicken bouillon cube, crushed

3 teaspoons Dijon mustard

1/2 teaspoon freshly grated nutmeg

1/2 teaspoon salt

10 cracks freshly ground black pepper

1 pound (450 g) Munster cheese, grated (4 cups)

1 cup (90 g) freshly grated Parmesan cheese

PREP

Generously butter baking dish. Preheat the oven to 350° F (180° C).

COOK

Bring milk and water to a boil in the saucepan, add the macaroni, and cook for half the amount of time required in package directions. Drain the macaroni in a sieve over a large bowl to catch the remaining liquid to use to make the sauce.

In the same saucepan, melt the butter, whisk in flour, and cook for 2 minutes. Slowly whisk in 3 cups (720 ml) of the reserved milk liquid from cooking the macaroni and keep whisking until thickened. Add the cream, bouillon cube, mustard, nutmeg, salt, pepper, and Munster cheese and vigorously stir to completely blend. Add the macaroni and stir to coat. At this point, taste for seasoning and add more salt, pepper, or nutmeg, if desired.

Scoop everything into the baking dish, top with Parmesan, and bake for 30–45 minutes.

IDEAS AND SUBSTITUTIONS

A light sprinkling of bread crumbs and dots of butter on the top before baking add a crunchy element to this creamy macaroni and cheese.

VEGETARIAN SHEPHERD'S PIE

Ratatouille Comme un Parmentier SERVES 6–8

Large enough to serve a family or a crowd, and even better the next day, this is my take on the classic French casserole, hachis parmentier, *which normally uses ground beef as its base layer before adding mashed potatoes on top and baking it.*

Having lived in the south of France for so long, I love the soft vegetable mixture invented in Nice, called ratatouille, *and substitute it for ground beef, which makes a lovely vegetable alternative base for the mashed potatoes that crown this rustic dish.*

SPECIAL EQUIPMENT 8 X 10-INCH (20 X 25-CM) CASSEROLE DISH; LARGE SAUCEPAN; POTATO RICER OR STAND MIXER; LARGE, WIDE POT; BAKING SHEET

6 tablespoons (90 ml) extra virgin olive oil, divided, plus enough to oil casserole dish

4 large cloves garlic

1 (6-ounce / 170-g) can tomato paste

3 to 4 teaspoons (20 to 30 g) all-purpose flour

4 medium russet potatoes, quartered

coarse sea salt and coarsely ground black pepper, plus more to garnish

4 tablespoons (60 g) unsalted butter, softened

1 1/2 cups (150 g) grated Gruyère or Emmental cheese, divided

1/2 cup (120 ml) milk

2 medium onions, peeled and thinly sliced

1 green bell pepper, coarsely chopped

4 medium zucchini, sliced vertically then into 1/4-inch (6-mm) slices

12 large fresh basil leaves, divided

3 sprigs fresh rosemary

2 sprigs fresh thyme

1 medium eggplant, coarsely chopped

1 medium carrot, coarsely grated

4 Roma tomatoes, thinly sliced

3 teaspoons sugar

PREP

Generously oil the casserole dish and preheat oven to 400° F (200 ° C).

Peel and finely chop 2 cloves garlic. Peel and finely slice the other 2 cloves. Mix tomato paste with flour.

COOK

Topping

Begin by putting the potatoes into the saucepan, cover with water, generously salt, bring to a boil, then reduce the heat, and cook until tender, about 20 minutes. Drain and when cool to the touch pull off the skins.

Put the potatoes through a ricer or beat them quickly in the stand mixer to break down. Add butter, 1/2 teaspoon salt, 1/4 teaspoon pepper, and 1/2 cup (50 g) cheese and beat until incorporated. Pour in enough of the milk to bring the potatoes to the consistency you like, adding more than called for if you want them to be lighter, although you need them to be thick enough to hold their shape when piled on top of the vegetables.

continued >

Filling

In the large pot, heat 4 tablespoons (60 ml) olive oil then add chopped garlic and onion and cook on medium for about 8 minutes. Add bell pepper and zucchini and stir. Add 8 torn basil leaves and some rosemary and thyme leaves then stir. Add eggplant, carrot, and tomatoes and stir. Stir in tomato paste mixture, the sliced garlic, and remaining olive oil and cook over low heat for 25 minutes, stirring frequently to turn the vegetables over. Taste and add salt and pepper, if you wish.

Transfer the ratatouille into the casserole dish and even the top. Sprinkle with remaining torn basil leaves. Top with big spoonfuls of mashed potatoes and swirl decoratively then evenly sprinkle the remaining cheese over the top. Give it all a sprinkle of coarse sea salt and coarsely ground pepper, place on the baking sheet, and bake for 30 minutes, or until bubbly and golden on top.

IDEAS AND SUBSTITUTIONS

If you have don't have fresh herbs, use a Bouquet Garni or dried herbs.

CHOPPED STEAK OVALS WITH ROQUEFORT COGNAC SAUCE

Steak Haché, Sauce au Cognac et au Roquefort SERVES 4

Almost a hamburger—but not quite. A steak haché *is prime steak coarsely ground then pressed into a flat oval shape, cooked, and then eaten like a steak rather than like a hamburger, without a bun or condiments. Chopped steak ovals present a low-cost alternative to steak. Paired with a lusciously rich Roquefort cognac cream sauce, it suddenly becomes a surprisingly luxurious meal.*

SPECIAL EQUIPMENT LARGE NONSTICK SKILLET

2 pounds (900 g) ground sirloin

1/2 pound (225 g) Roquefort cheese, room temperature

1 teaspoon kosher salt

8 cracks coarsely ground black pepper

all-purpose flour for dredging

3 tablespoons (45 ml) extra virgin olive oil, divided

2 medium shallots, peeled and minced

1/3 cup (80 ml) half-and-half

dash cayenne pepper

2 tablespoons (30 ml) cognac

PREP

Shape the ground steak into 4 flat ovals. Mash the Roquefort with a fork.

COOK

Liberally salt and pepper the steak ovals then dredge in flour and shake off excess. Heat 2 table-spoons (30 ml) olive oil in the skillet and fry the steak ovals over high heat for 3 minutes on each side for medium-rare. Remove the steak ovals to dinner plates.

In the same skillet, heat remaining olive oil over medium heat. Add the shallots and stir while they cook for 2 minutes. Add the half-and-half, Roquefort, and cayenne and stir, bringing the sauce to a boil. Reduce the heat and whisk vigorously until the cheese is melted. Remove from the heat, pour in the cognac, and whisk.

To serve, ladle sauce over one half and around each steak oval.

IDEAS AND SUBSTITUTIONS

Grind your own meat by placing chunks of sirloin into your food processor and pulsing until you have coarsely ground steak. This way you can control the quality of the steaks and their texture.

SUCCULENT ROAST CHICKEN WITH ORANGES AND BLACK OLIVES

Succulent Poulet Rôti à l'Orange et aux Olives Noires SERVES 4-6

When I lived on the Rue Saint-Jean-Baptiste de la Salle in Paris and walked down my street on a Sunday, the smell of chickens cooking would swirl around in the noontime air making me crazy with hunger by the time I reached the end of the street. It seemed that Sunday chicken was de rigueur *with the concierges living in the ground floor apartments, which they would simmer in stews or roast in the oven.*

I learned this version of the classic Sunday roast chicken while later living on the Riviera, where orange and olive trees thrive, making it a natural and healthy combination and an absolutely delicious Sunday chicken.

SPECIAL EQUIPMENT MICROPLANE OR ZESTER; FOOD PROCESSOR OR BLENDER; ROASTING PAN WITH ROASTER RACK

1 organic medium-size orange

4 tablespoons (60 ml) extra virgin olive oil

4 large cloves garlic, peeled and minced

2 tablespoons fresh tarragon leaves

12 leaves flat-leaf parsley

2 teaspoons herbes de Provence

4 tablespoons (80 g) orange marmalade

18 oil-cured black olives, pitted, divided

1 (5 to 6-pound / 2.3 to 2.5-kg) free-range roasting chicken

1 cup (240 ml) chicken stock

PREP

Preheat oven to 400° F (200 ° C). Zest and juice the orange, reserving the leftover rinds.

COOK

In the food processor, add olive oil, orange zest, garlic, tarragon, parsley, herbes de Provence, 1 tablespoon orange juice, marmalade, and 10 olives. Process 60 seconds until it makes a paste.

Slip your fingers under the skin of the breast meat of the chicken and generously slather some of the mixture inside. Settle the chicken on the roasting rack in the roasting pan, and then slather the entire exterior of the bird with the paste, allowing any extra to slide off to the bottom of the roasting pan. Stuff the cavity with the leftover rinds of the orange.

Add the rest of the orange juice, chicken stock, and remaining olives to the bottom of the roasting pan.

Bake for 1 hour and 30 minutes, or until the internal temperature reaches 165° F (74° C). Transfer the chicken to a serving platter to rest while you place the roasting pan on the stove over low heat. Add a little water to the pan, and with a wooden spoon, scrape off the bits from the bottom of the pan and stir until you make gravy. Serve with the chicken.

IDEAS AND SUGGESTIONS

Instead of water, you can add wine to the bottom of the pan when making the gravy.

ENDIVES AND HAM GRATIN

Gratin d'Endives au Jambon SERVES 4

Although Belgians lay a valid claim to the origin of this dish, it is a firm family favorite throughout France as a warming winter dish—especially on a gray cold day when rain is pounding on the windows and children need warming up.

To make it, whole endives are wrapped in a slice of ham then baked in a casserole with a Mornay sauce to create a cozy meal.

SPECIAL EQUIPMENT LARGE SKILLET; 9 X 12-INCH (23 X 30-CM) CASSEROLE OR GRATIN DISH; SAUCEPAN; ALUMINUM FOIL

- 4 tablespoons (60 g) unsalted butter, plus more to butter casserole dish
- 8 large endives
- 2 to 4 tablespoons (30 to 60 ml) olive oil
- 1 to 2 tablespoons (15 to 30 g) sugar
- 8 large, thin slices boiled ham

- 4 tablespoons (30 g) all-purpose flour
- 2 cups milk (480 ml) or fat-free half-and-half
- 4 teaspoons Dijon mustard
- 1/2 teaspoon freshly grated nutmeg
- 1/4 teaspoon salt

- 6 cracks freshly ground black pepper
- 1 clove garlic, peeled and minced
- 8 ounces (225 g) Jarlsburg, Gruyère, Emmental, or French Cantal cheese, grated
- 1/2 cup (45 g) grated Parmesan cheese

PREP

Generously butter the casserole dish and preheat the oven to 450° F (230° C).

Clean the endives, pull off any discolored outer leaves, slice the root end off, and slice in half lengthwise.

COOK

Add 2 tablespoons (30 ml) olive oil to the skillet and heat until very hot. Sprinkle with 1 tablespoon sugar then arrange as many endive halves as you can in the skillet and cook for about 3 minutes, until nicely browned. Turn over and cook the other side until nicely browned. Remove to a plate and repeat with the remaining endives, adding more oil and another tablespoon of sugar, if needed.

Put 2 endive halves back together to make a whole endive, roll in a piece of ham, and repeat with the remaining endives.

In the saucepan, melt the butter, whisk in the flour, then very slowly whisk in milk over medium heat until the sauce thickens and bubbles. Add mustard, nutmeg, salt, pepper, garlic, and cheese of choice and whisk until melted and well blended to make your sauce. Add a little more milk if you would like it a bit thinner.

Pour some of the sauce in the bottom of the casserole dish, arrange the endives rolls in the dish, pour the rest of the sauce over them, sprinkle the Parmesan over the top, and then add a generous sprinkling of salt and coarsely ground black pepper.

Cover the dish with aluminum foil and bake for 20 minutes. Remove the foil and bake another 25 minutes, until the top is golden and bubbly. Remove from the oven and cool a little before serving as it will be very hot.

IDEAS AND SUBSTITUTIONS

You can make this dish without the ham for a vegetarian version and it is equally delicious.

SLOW-COOKER LAMB SHANKS PROVENÇAL

Daube de Souris d'Agneau à la Provençale SERVES 4

Plates with egg noodles or mashed potatoes heaped in the center, dramatically topped with a whole lamb shank that has been cooked until fork-tender, and surrounded by an impeccable sauce fortified with vegetables, can easily be prepared as a weeknight family dinner if you follow this recipe made in a slow cooker. There's even enough sauce leftover to ladle over pasta the next day.

SPECIAL EQUIPMENT 6 ½-QUART (6-L) SLOW COOKER; LARGE SKILLET; 4 DINNER PLATES

1 medium onion

small bunch fresh parsley

6 large cloves garlic, peeled and thinly sliced

1 medium carrot, sliced into ¼-inch (6-mm) pieces

2 medium tomatoes, coarsely chopped

1 organic lemon, zested

2 cups (480 ml) chicken stock

2 cups (480 ml) dry red wine

1 teaspoon salt, plus more to taste

1 (6-ounce / 170-g) can tomato paste

1 tablespoon honey

3 tablespoons (45 ml) cognac

1 tablespoon herbes de Provence

coarsely ground black pepper, to taste

all-purpose flour for dredging

4 lamb shanks (make sure they are short enough to fit in your slow cooker)

4 tablespoons (60 ml) extra virgin olive oil

1 (14-ounce / 400-g) can artichoke hearts, drained and patted dry

8 oil-cured black olives, pitted and cut into small pieces

mashed potatoes or cooked egg noodles

PREP

Slice the onion in half, peel, slice in half again, and then slice into ¼-inch (6-mm) pieces. Slice stems off parsley and finely chop the leaves. Discard stems.

COOK

Put the onion, garlic, carrot, tomatoes, lemon zest, stock, wine, salt, tomato paste, honey, cognac, and herbs de Provence in the slow cooker.

Salt and pepper lamb shanks and lightly dredge in flour. In the skillet on high heat, brown the shanks on all sides in the olive oil. Arrange in slow cooker. Cover and cook for 6 hours on high, or low for 8–10 hours. Halfway through cooking time, turn the shanks over and ladle with sauce.

One hour before the dish is finished cooking, add the artichoke hearts and olives, take the lid off, and place it at an angle over the slow cooker to allow evaporation of some of the liquid.

To serve, mound mashed potatoes or noodles in the center of each plate. Place 1 lamb shank on top of each plate and ladle the vegetables and some of the liquid from the slow cooker over each shank. Sprinkle with parsley and serve.

IDEAS AND SUBSTITUTIONS

There should be enough delicious lamb-flavored broth left to make either a soup or use as a base for a sauce the next day.

POTATO, BACON, CHEESE, AND WINE CASSEROLE

La Tartiflette SERVES 6

High in the Haute-Savoie region of the French Alps, chalets and village restaurants prepare this dish on wintery nights. With its potatoes, cheese, bacon, onions, and wine, it has to be one of the most comforting of all potato dishes.

To be authentic, try to locate Reblochon cheese and a French Savoie wine to use for the casserole. Otherwise Gruyère, Raclette, Pont l'Évêque, or Brie work well.

SPECIAL EQUIPMENT 9 X 9-INCH (23 X 23-CM) OR 9 X 10-INCH (23 X 25-CM) OVEN-PROOF BAKING DISH OR INDIVIDUAL RAMEKINS; LARGE SAUCEPAN; LARGE SKILLET; MEDIUM SKILLET

2 large cloves garlic

butter or duck fat to grease the baking dish

2½ pounds (1.2 kg) Idaho or russet potatoes, peeled and sliced in half

1 tablespoon extra virgin olive oil

1 large onion, peeled, cut into quarters, then thinly sliced

½ pound (225 g) thick-cut bacon, sliced into ½-inch (1.5-cm) pieces

salt and coarsely ground black pepper, to taste

¾ cup (180 ml) heavy cream

½ cup (120 ml) dry white wine

1 pound (450 g) Reblochon, Gruyère, Swiss, Raclette, or Pont l'Eveque cheese, cut into thick slices

PREP

Peel garlic, mince 1 clove, and slice the other in half. Rub the halves of garlic all over the inside of the baking dish then liberally grease with either butter or duck fat.

Preheat oven to 350° F (180° C).

COOK

Place the potatoes in the saucepan, cover with water, bring to a boil, then reduce heat, and cook until a knife can be inserted easily, about 14 minutes. Cool to room temperature then thinly slice.

Heat the olive oil in the large skillet and add the onion and minced garlic. Cook for 10–12 minutes on medium until light golden brown. At the same time, in the other skillet, cook the bacon until crisp. Transfer the bacon, plus 1 tablespoon of bacon fat to the skillet with the onion and mix well to combine.

Arrange a layer of overlapping potatoes in the bottom of the baking dish. Liberally sprinkle salt and pepper over the top, and then layer on all of the bacon and onion mixture. Arrange another layer of potatoes over the top, liberally salt and pepper, and pour the cream then the wine over the potatoes.

Layer the cheese slices over the top and bake for 30 minutes. Turn off the oven and allow the casserole to rest for 10 minutes in the oven. Serve with a crisp white wine and green salad.

IDEAS AND SUBSTITUTIONS

I also love using Brie cheese for this dish. Buy 2 (8-ounce / 230-g) wheels; gently scrape off the rind then slice both in half horizontally. Place the 4 rounds on top of the casserole before it goes into the oven to bake.

This casserole can be put together several hours ahead and baked just before serving.

QUICK BEEF AND RED WINE STEW OVER NOODLES

Bœuf Bourguignon Rapide SERVES 4

A stew from the Burgundy region in eastern France, bœuf Bourguignon *is slowly braised until fork tender—a mixture of beef, wine, and vegetables that is one of the most iconic and best-loved dishes in French cuisine.*

Mine shouldn't take much longer than 30–40 minutes to prepare and pretty closely approximates the authentic longer cooking version.

SPECIAL EQUIPMENT DUTCH OVEN OR LARGE SOUP POT

2 pounds (900 g) beef tenderloin or beef tenderloin tips

½ cup (60 g) all-purpose flour, plus 2 tablespoons

salt and coarsely ground black pepper, to taste

¼ pound (110 g) bacon or good slab bacon, sliced into ½-inch (1.5-cm) pieces

olive oil

1 medium onion, peeled and finely chopped

1 (16-ounce / 450-g) package frozen pearl onions, thawed

4 cloves garlic, peeled and minced

1½ teaspoons thyme (fresh or dried)

4 cups (1 l) Burgundy or dry red wine, plus a little extra

1½ pounds (700 g) button mushrooms, sliced in half

cooked egg noodles

PREP

Cut beef into large chunks, 1 to 1½-inch (2.5 to 4-cm) pieces, and pat dry with paper towels. Try to make them identical in size so they cook evenly. Place ½ cup (60 g) flour on a plate and liberally season with salt and lots of coarsely ground black pepper.

COOK

In the Dutch oven, cook the bacon on medium heat until golden brown. Remove to paper towels and set aside. Dredge the beef chunks in the flour and shake off excess.

In the Dutch oven, heat the bacon grease until shimmering hot, add a layer of the beef chunks, and brown on all sides, leaving the insides rare. Remove to a plate and repeat with the remaining beef, adding some olive oil, if needed.

In the Dutch oven, cook the chopped onion and the pearl onions until golden brown. Add the garlic,

thyme, and wine and bring to a simmer. Remove 1 cup (240 ml) of the sauce, mix in the 2 tablespoons (15 g) flour with a fork, return to the Dutch oven, and simmer again, stirring until the sauce thickens. If it is too thick, add a little more wine. Add the mushrooms, bring back to a simmer, and cook for 4 minutes.

Return the beef to the Dutch oven and cook for about 1 minute, just long enough to reheat the meat. Test one piece to see if it is done to your liking. If you would like it well done, cook longer. Add in the bacon and stir. Serve over egg noodles.

IDEAS AND SUGGESTIONS

You can dress up this dish by sprinkling freshly chopped parsley over the top and serving it with a simple arugula salad. A small dash of cognac stirred into the sauce at the end is also lovely.

CHICKEN MARENGO

Poulet Marengo SERVES 4

Allegedly created in honor of Napoleon's victory over the Austrians at the Battle of Marengo in 1800, the original recipe for chicken Marengo is said to have included crayfish, eggs, and truffles.

Today there are so many versions of the dish that it seems the only unifying factor is that it is made with chicken! By far, the way I've been served it the most is with tomatoes, onions, mushrooms, wine, and sometimes with a fried egg on toast on the side. I prefer to serve mine on noodles, without the crayfish or truffles.

SPECIAL EQUIPMENT LARGE NONSTICK SKILLET; LARGE POT OR DUTCH OVEN

- 2 tablespoons (15 g) all-purpose flour, plus flour for dredging chicken
- 1½ cups (260 ml) dry white wine or Madeira
- 5 tablespoons (75 ml) cognac, divided
- 2 tablespoons (335 g) tomato paste
- 1 teaspoon salt
- ½ teaspoon freshly ground pepper
- 1 teaspoon sugar
- pinch ground nutmeg
- 2 slices bacon, coarsely chopped
- 12 boneless chicken thighs, skin on
- 1 tablespoon (15 ml) extra virgin olive oil
- 1 large shallot, peeled and chopped
- 5 large cloves garlic, peeled and chopped
- 2 medium Roma tomatoes, coarsely chopped
- 20 cherry tomatoes
- 2 tablespoons coarsely chopped fresh basil and thyme
- 16 small button mushrooms
- cooked noodles

PREP

Whisk together the 2 tablespoons (15 g) flour, wine, 4 tablespoons (60 ml) cognac, tomato paste, salt, pepper, sugar, and nutmeg.

COOK

In the skillet, cook the bacon until crisp then add to the pot. Reserve the bacon fat.

Generously season chicken with salt and pepper on both sides and lightly dredge in flour. Brown the chicken in the bacon fat until golden, for about 3 minutes per side, then add to the pot.

Add the olive oil to the skillet and cook the shallots and garlic for 3 minutes then add to the pot.

Toss the tomatoes and whole cherry tomatoes into the pot and pour in the wine mixture. Cover and bring to a boil then reduce to medium-low heat and cook for 10 minutes. Check that the chicken is done to your liking and cook longer, if needed. Just before serving, stir in remaining cognac, and mix well. Serve over noodles.

IDEAS AND SUBSTITUTIONS

If you don't want to use wine, use chicken stock as a substitute. If you have fresh basil around, it is a lovely addition chopped into the sauce.

This freezes well if you want to make it on a weekend and have leftovers later in the week.

NORMANDY PORK CHOPS WITH APPLE BRANDY CREAM SAUCE AND APPLE COMPOTE

Côtes de Porc à la Normande, Compote de Pommes SERVES 4

There's a cider route called La Route de Cidre *you can follow in Normandy's Pays d'Auge that guides you through apple orchards, past half-timbered houses, châteaux, and meanders by meadows filled with bovine beauties. This is where they make apple cider, apple brandy called Calvados, and apple-inspired dishes which include butter, cream, and cheese from the cows.*

For this recipe from Normandy, you will need to find dry hard cider, called cidre buché, *(cider under cork) and Calvados or apple brandy. A soupçon of cream for the sauce, a side of tangy apple compote for the pork, and you can serve a charming meal from the very heart of Normandy.*

SPECIAL EQUIPMENT WIDE SOUP POT OR LARGE WIDE SAUCEPAN WITH LID; LARGE SKILLET; MEAT THERMOMETER; SMALL SAUCEPAN; 4 DINNER PLATES

Apple Compote

¼ cup (50 g) sugar, plus 2 tablespoons

¼ teaspoon salt

4 tablespoons (60 ml) apple brandy or Calvados, divided

6 large Granny Smith apples, unpeeled, sliced into ½-inch (1.5-cm) chunks

Pork Chops

4 (8-ounce / 225-g) ½-inch-thick (1.5-cm) bone-in pork chops, room temperature

¼ cup (60 g) all-purpose flour

kosher salt and coarsely ground black pepper, to taste

4 tablespoons (60 ml) extra virgin olive oil

½ cup (120 ml) apple brandy or Calvados

½ cup (120 ml) semidry or extra dry hard cider

¼ teaspoon salt

4 cracks coarsely ground black pepper

5 tablespoons (75 g) heavy cream

PREP FOR PORK CHOPS

Rinse and pat dry the pork chops. Generously season the flour with salt and coarsely ground black pepper.

COOK

Apple Compote

In the soup pot, melt ¼ cup (50 g) sugar and salt with 3 tablespoons (45 ml) brandy. Add the apples and stir well to evenly coat with the sugar syrup. Cover and cook on medium heat for 10 minutes until the apples are soft, stirring frequently. Take the lid off, sprinkle with remaining sugar and

brandy, and stir while the mixture cooks for another 4 minutes, mashing some of the apple chunks with a fork. Remove from the heat and keep covered until ready to use.

Pork Chops

Liberally salt and pepper the pork chops, lightly dredge them in the flour, and shake off excess.

In the skillet, heat the olive oil until it shimmers then add the pork chops and fry them on medium-high heat until golden brown and crispy, about 2–3 minutes. Turn over and fry the other side until golden brown, crispy, and the meat thermometer

continued >

registers 140° F (60 ° C). Remove to a plate and take the skillet off the heat.

Heat the brandy in the small saucepan, step back from the pan, and ignite liquor. Let the flame die then pour into the skillet.

Put the skillet back on medium heat and, with a wooden spoon, scrape the cooked bits from the bottom of the pan. Add the cider, ¼ teaspoon salt, and 4 cracks coarsely ground black pepper and bring to a boil; let cook down for 3 minutes. Pour in the cream and bring to a boil. Reduce to a simmer and cook for 2 minutes.

Place 1 pork chop on each plate and divide the sauce evenly over the top. Spoon apple compote to one side and serve.

IDEAS AND SUBSTITUTIONS

You can crumble in pieces of Normandy camembert to cook down with the cream in the sauce for added richness.

Pears instead of apples can be used to make the compote.

SLOW-COOKER LAYERED MEATS AND POTATO CASSEROLE FROM ALSACE

Le Baeckeoffe Alsacien SERVES 6

Baeckeoffe is a many-layered meat stew made in Alsace, typically on Sundays. The meats are marinated overnight and baked the next day in a terra cotta clay casserole with a lid sealed with dough. The word baeckeoffe means baker's oven, referring to the fact that people would drop their casseroles off at the village baker the evening before so that it would be baked in his oven for them to pick up the next day for dinner. Their slowly cooked casseroles were laden with a harmony of mutton, pork, and beef soaked in wine and juniper berries, supplemented by potatoes, onions, leeks, and herbs. It was the baker's personal touch to seal their casseroles with a braiding of dough while the casseroles baked.

I love this one-pot dinner and learned to make it in a slow cooker—without the dough seal.

SPECIAL EQUIPMENT MORTAR AND PESTLE OR SMALL FOOD PROCESSOR; LARGE STOCK POT; LARGE SKILLET; 6 ½-QUART (6-L) SLOW COOKER

- 1 tablespoon juniper berries
- 1 ½ pounds (675 g) beef chuck roast, cut into 1-inch (2.5-cm) cubes
- 1 ½ pounds (675 g) boneless pork shoulder or butt, cut into 1-inch (2.5-cm) cubes
- ½ pound (225 g) lamb shoulder or stewing lamb, cut into 1-inch (2.5-cm) cubes

- 1 large yellow onion, peeled, sliced in quarters, and then thinly sliced
- 4 cloves garlic, peeled and thinly sliced
- 6 large carrots, sliced into ¼-inch (6-mm) rounds
- 2 medium leeks, white and pale green parts sliced into ¼-inch (6-mm) rounds
- 2 whole cloves

- 3 cups (720 ml) Riesling or Sauvignon Blanc or dry white wine
- salt and coarsely ground black pepper, to taste
- all-purpose flour for dredging meats
- 2 tablespoons (30 ml) olive oil
- 2 ½ pounds (1.2 kg) Yukon gold potatoes
- ½ tablespoon cornstarch

PREP

Coarsely crush juniper berries in a mortar and pestle or small food processor.

COOK

Put the cubes of meat, onion, garlic, carrots, leeks, juniper berries, cloves, and wine in the large pot, cover, and marinate overnight in the refrigerator.

The next day, remove the cloves and the meat from the marinade and reserve the marinade. Reserve the vegetables.

Pat the meats dry with paper towels and liberally season with salt and coarsely ground black pepper. Heat olive oil in the skillet on high heat until it is shimmering hot. Pour some flour on a large plate and season with salt and pepper. Dredge the meat in the flour, shake off excess, and then brown on all sides in skillet. As the meats brown, add them to the slow cooker. When all the meat is browned, deglaze the skillet with 1 cup (240 ml) of the marinade, scraping up the bits on the bottom of the skillet. Pour everything into the slow cooker.

Add all the marinated vegetables on top of the meat in the slow cooker. Cut the potatoes, skin on, in half, then into ¼-inch (6-mm) half-moon slices and arrange over the vegetable layer in the slow cooker.

Mix the cornstarch into the remaining marinade, pour over the top, and add another ½ cup (120 ml) of any kind of wine you have around. Season with salt and coarsely ground black pepper, pop the lid on, and cook on low for 6 hours. Serve with Dijon mustard and slices of baguette.

CHICKEN IN WINE WITH LOADS OF GARLIC

Poulet au Vin Avec Beaucoup d'Ail SERVES 4

There used to be a restaurant in Lyon called Chez Tante Paulette, run by Marie-Louise Auteli. I learned about her from reading Patricia Wells' Food Lover's Guide to France and began visiting her establishment for her Chicken with 40 Cloves of Garlic. She loved her garlic. This dish was amazing, as was her Garlic Salad, a simple mixture of greens with freshly minced garlic scattered on top.

One night after dinner in her tiny restaurant, she came out to sit with us at the table to talk about food and visit. Tiny as a bird, she sipped a thimbleful of red wine and laughed a good deal. Those golden memories simmer together within my rendition of her famous dish. She is no longer there to visit or share wine with, but I hope I am honoring her in continuing her tradition of pairing "loads of garlic" with chicken.

SPECIAL EQUIPMENT LARGE SKILLET; DUTCH OVEN OR LARGE SOUP POT WITH LID

2 whole heads garlic

2 sprigs fresh rosemary

4 sprigs fresh thyme

8 boneless chicken thighs, skin on, room temperature

kosher salt and freshly ground black pepper, to taste

all-purpose flour for dredging

olive oil

3 cups (720 ml) dry white wine

1 to 2 cups (240 to 480 ml) chicken broth

cooked noodles

PREP

Separate the heads of garlic into cloves, peel them, and slice. Pull the leaves off the rosemary and 2 of the thyme sprigs, discard stems, and coarsely chop the rosemary and thyme leaves. Reserve 2 whole thyme sprigs.

COOK

Rinse the chicken under running water, pat dry with paper towels, and liberally season with salt and pepper. Dredge in flour generously seasoned with salt and pepper and shake off excess. Add olive oil to the skillet, heat until shimmering hot, and brown the chicken on both sides. Transfer the chicken pieces to the Dutch oven, tuck in the sprigs of thyme, and scatter the thyme and rosemary leaves over the top.

Cook the garlic in the same skillet until golden. Add half the wine and scrape the bottom of the skillet with a wooden spoon to bring up the browned bits. Pour into the Dutch oven, add the rest of the wine, and top up with chicken broth, if needed, to cover the chicken.

Partially cover and cook for 20 minutes or until done. Salt and pepper, to taste. Serve over noodles.

IDEAS AND SUBSTITUTIONS

I love the simplicity of this dish and would not change a thing. However, variations I have tasted include adding pearl onions and mushrooms.

RIB-STICKING PORK AND VEGETABLE STEW WITH GIANT DUMPLINGS

Mique et Porc en Pot-au-Feu Réconfortant

SERVES 4 WITH 4 GIANT DUMPLINGS OR 6 WITH 20–30 SMALL DUMPLINGS

A pot-au-feu, (pot on the fire), is different than other meat stews in France in that it produces a two-for-one meal: you first ladle out the broth and serve it as a soup, perhaps with some croutons, and then serve a main course of the boiled meat, vegetables, and dumplings with sides of mustard and cornichons. The slow-cooking technique on the back burner of the stove for a couple of hours creates a harmonious marriage of flavors worthy of warming the coldest night.

There are many variations of pot-au-feu in France. In the Périgord region, they are likely to make it with duck and/or foie gras *and include large dumplings called* miques. *The dumplings are something that villagers make with leftover bread and eggs that gently cook in the broth of the stew. Most families and villages have their own variation of these dumplings, some making them small and some so large they take up half the plate. For this pot-au-feu, I like to use a mixture of pork and beef marrow bones rather than duck, and make my dumplings very large. The dumplings are normally sliced and used like bread, but I also like to serve slices of warm baguette to sop up the broth as well.*

You can make the pot-au-feu a day ahead to allow the flavors to deepen then make the dumplings the day you wish to serve it.

SPECIAL EQUIPMENT VERY LARGE SOUP POT; MEDIUM SAUCEPAN; LARGE PLATE; LARGE POT OR DEEP SKILLET

Stew

2 medium leeks

2 small onions

4 whole cloves

6 large carrots

4 stalks celery with leaves

3 medium potatoes

6 fingerling potatoes

small bunch fresh flat-leaf parsley

3 pounds (1.350 kg) pork butt

2 tablespoons (30 ml) extra virgin olive oil

2 beef marrow bones

3 bay leaves

1 teaspoon whole peppercorns

2 teaspoons sea salt

6 cracks freshly ground black pepper

2 sprigs fresh rosemary or 2 teaspoons dried

8 cloves garlic, peeled and thinly sliced

8 cups (2 l) chicken stock

6 links pork sausages, sliced in half or 1 Kielbasa, sliced into 2-inch (5-cm) pieces

1 small cabbage, trimmed and thinly sliced

Dijon or whole grain mustard, cornichons, and sliced baguette

Dumplings

¼ cup (30 g) flour

3 teaspoons baking powder

1 cup (250 ml) pot-au-feu broth

1 cup (250 ml) water

1 teaspoon kosher salt

6 cracks coarsely ground black pepper

4 large cloves garlic, peeled and minced

1 tablespoon (15 ml) extra virgin olive oil

1½ loaves (2 pounds / 900 g), stale white bread sliced into very small cubes

3 tablespoons minced fresh parsley

¼ cup (40 g) cornmeal

5 large eggs, beaten

continued >

PREP FOR STEW

Trim leeks, leaving 2 inches (5 cm) of the green. Slice in half vertically to clean the insides under running water then slice into 2-inch (5-cm) pieces. Peel onions, slice into quarters, and stud 4 of the quarters with cloves.

Clean and thinly slice 2 carrots and peel and slice 4 carrots in 2-inch (5-cm) pieces. Thinly slice 2 stalks celery and slice the remaining 2 stalks into 2-inch (5-cm) pieces. Keep the leaves.

Peel the potatoes, cut into equal 1 to 2-inch (2.5 to 5-cm) slices, and reserve in a bowl of cold water. Remove leaves from parsley and finely chop leaves. Finely chop stems and reserve.

PREP FOR DUMPLINGS

Sieve the flour and baking powder together into a bowl.

COOK

Stew

In the soup pot, brown the pork in olive oil. Add the marrow bones, leeks, onions, carrots, celery, celery leaves, bay leaves, peppercorns, salt, ground pepper, rosemary, garlic, chopped parsley stems, and stock then top up with water, if needed, to cover the meat. Put a cover on, bring to a boil, then reduce to a simmer, and cook, uncovered, for 2 hours, skimming off any gray scum that forms on the top.

When the pork is done, take it out and place on a cutting board. Add the cabbage, potatoes, and sausages to the pot-au-feu, submerge in the liquid, and cook until the potatoes become fork tender. During the time the potatoes are cooking you can prepare the dumplings.

Dumplings

In the saucepan, heat the broth, water, salt, pepper, garlic, and olive oil to a simmer.

Place the cubed bread in a large bowl, pour the hot broth mixture over them, and toss to thoroughly coat. Allow to rest for 12 minutes.

Evenly shake the flour mixture, parsley, and cornmeal over the bread cubes and toss with a fork to coat.

Add the eggs, and with floured hands, bring the mixture together into dumplings, either giant ones or small ones. You can add more of the broth, if needed, to bring them together, or more flour if needed. Shape into 4 giant dumplings or 20–30 smaller ones. Place dumplings on the plate, cover with a towel, and place in the refrigerator for 35 minutes. Meanwhile, bring at least 4 inches (10 cm) of water to a boil in the large pot. Reduce to a simmer and slip the dumplings in to poach for anywhere from 40–45 minutes for giant dumplings, to 25–35 minutes for small ones, turning them over several times so they cook on all sides. When sliced, they should be spongy inside. Remove dumplings with a slotted spoon.

When the dumplings are cooked, remove the bay leaves and whole cloves from the pot-au-feu and discard. To serve, ladle soup into bowls and offer as a soup course, or save for another meal. I often skip the soup course and plate everything with some of the broth in shallow bowls as follows: slice the meat and divide between the bowls then surround it with the vegetables, potatoes, a dumpling, and a little of the broth poured over everything. Scatter the chopped parsley over the top.

Don't forget to put the mustard and cornichons, sea salt and a pepper mill on the table! The mustard is particularly good spread on the dumplings and tasted with the meat and cornichons.

IDEAS AND SUBSTITUTIONS

If I can find it, I love to add to the stew a slice or two of pork belly along with the pork and marrow bones for added flavor.

If you have a vegetable garden, pull up the smallest carrots or baby turnips, clean them, leave on a couple of inches of stem, and cook them with the cabbage the last half hour. They add a lovely look and fresh taste to the pot-au-feu.

CREAMLESS CREAMY VEAL STEW WITH MUSHROOMS AND PEARL ONIONS

Blanquette de Veau aux Champignons et aux Oignons Grelots SERVES 6

One of the most monochrome dishes you could ever eat, a blanquette de veau *is a heavenly dish where chunks of veal are slowly simmered in wine and water before coming together with a creamy sauce, mushrooms, and pearl onions. Normally made with a* velouté *(velvet) sauce (stock thickened with flour and butter) enriched with egg yolk, heavy cream, and lemon juice, I make mine lighter and without cream—yet it has the same creamy taste and silky texture.*

The lineage of blanquette de veau is long, having first appeared in the very first public restaurants in Paris after the French Revolution. Although traditionally made with veal, a blanquette can also be made with chicken, turkey, or lamb. It's a calming, comforting dish that soothes when soothing is needed.

SPECIAL EQUIPMENT LARGE SOUP POT; LARGE DUTCH OVEN OR COVERED POT; FINE SIEVE; LARGE SKILLET; MEDIUM SAUCEPAN

4 stalks celery with leaves

4 pounds (2.8 kg) veal stew meat or veal shoulder, sliced into 1½ to 2-inch (4 to 5-cm) pieces

4 cups (1 l) chicken stock

3 cups (720 ml) dry white wine, plus a little more to thin the sauce, if needed

2 sprigs fresh thyme

2 bay leaves

3 medium carrots, grated

1 medium onion, sliced in half, studded with 5 cloves

2 cloves garlic, peeled and minced

3 tablespoons (23 g) extra virgin olive oil, plus more to fry onions and mushrooms

1 (16-ounce / 450-g) package frozen pearl onions, thawed

1 pound (450 g) button mushrooms or a mixture of wild mushrooms, sliced

3 tablespoons (23 g) all-purpose flour

½ cup (120 ml) fat-free half-and-half

2 large egg yolks, room temperature, beaten

½ lemon, juiced

salt and freshly ground black pepper, to taste

boiled potatoes or cooked noodles, sprinkled with chopped parsley, optional

PREP

Clean and finely chop the celery. Reserve the leaves and chop.

COOK

Drop the veal into a pot of boiling water and blanch for 5 minutes. Remove the veal with a slotted spoon and transfer to the Dutch oven, adding the stock, wine, thyme, bay leaves, carrots, and onion with cloves. Add water, if needed, to cover the meat. Bring to a boil then turn the heat down to low and cook, partially covered, for 1½ hours, until fork tender.

Remove from the heat then remove the bay leaves. With a slotted spoon, transfer the veal to a plate. Strain the broth through the sieve into a bowl and reserve. Discard what is in the sieve.

Fry the pearl onions and mushrooms in olive oil over medium high heat until golden.

In the saucepan, heat 3 tablespoons (45 ml) olive oil, whisk in flour, and cook for 2 minutes on medium low. Slowly pour in 3 cups (720 ml) of the reserved veal broth (top up with wine, if needed, to make 3 cups), turn heat up to medium, and cook until the sauce has thickened. Whisk in the half-and-half.

Pour ¼ cup (60 ml) of the sauce into the egg yolks and whisk until combined then pour into the saucepan with the sauce and vigorously whisk for 1 minute. Add the lemon juice and whisk to combine. Add a little more white wine to thin the sauce, if needed. Taste and add salt and freshly ground black pepper.

Add the veal and any juices on the plate, pearl onions, and mushrooms to the sauce, stir, and heat, if needed. Serve with boiled potatoes or over noodles and sprinkle with the celery leaves.

IDEAS AND SUGGESTIONS

Veer off the traditional combination by fortifying the recipe with peas and carrots. It can also be used as a great base for a pot pie.

SUPPER FOR FRIENDS

A s a prelude to starting a weekend or as a way to enjoy a midweek break, entertaining friends at home is the way I slow down, especially so when life becomes hectic.

During the week, I'll ask a close friend to help by coming by early to light the fire or uncork the wine, another to bring a fresh baguette, and the arriving guests to settle in and relax. My menu could be as simple as pasta or a roast chicken I bought on the way home, a slow-cooker *cassoulet* I made on Sunday and serve on Tuesday, a barbecue in the garden during the summer, or a simple cheese fondue in the winter. It's all about spending time together, good conversation, and carving out a couple of hours at the end of the day to unwind and have fun. With meals that are practically effortless and close friends who are just happy to be together (and usually help do the dishes), entertaining during the week is totally possible and totally French.

On weekends, I like to entertain on a Sunday night and make it more of a special event. There may be new faces at the table and more than one course, with dishes that I love to cook that take more time than I have to spare during the week or that lend themselves to bringing out my best china and wines.

While others have parties where the focus is entertainment, the French entertain by inviting friends for supper, where the entertainment is food. The following recipes are a mix of quick weeknight dinners and more elegant weekend meals you can make for French-inspired entertaining at home.

FRENCH ALPS CHEESE FONDUE

La Fondue Savoyarde SERVES 4

Many snow-covered chalets in the Savoie region of the French Alps offer après-ski *food by the fireplace for their guests. The most popular is cheese fondue because it is a communal dish that gathers people around one bubbling pot of melted cheese to dip their chunks of bread and share stories about their day on the slopes.*

Depending on where you are in the French Alps, fondue may be made with Reblochon, Beaufort, Tomme de Savoie, Comté, Abondance, or French Gruyère cheese—served along with a dry white vin de Savoie, *such as Aspremont. If you are not able to locate these cheeses where you live, simply choose ones you love and substitute. It's all about the sharing and the love of melted cheese!*

SPECIAL EQUIPMENT BOX GRATER; LARGE FONDUE POT OVER FLAME OR LARGE CHAFING DISH OVER FLAME; LARGE SAUCEPAN; FONDUE LONG FORKS

2 cloves garlic

8 ounces (225 g) Gruyère cheese

8 ounces (225 g) Comté, Emmenthaler, or Raclette cheese

1 long French baguette or large farmhouse rustic loaf

2 cups (480 ml) dry white wine, plus extra to thin cheese, if needed

½ teaspoon freshly grated nutmeg

1½ tablespoons all-purpose flour

¼ cup (60 ml) Kirsch (cherry liqueur)

PREP

Peel the garlic and slice one in half. Mince the other. Coarsely grate cheeses on the large holes of a box grater. Slice bread into large cubes and pile in a bowl or basket.

COOK

Wipe the garlic halves all over the interior of the fondue pot.

In the saucepan, heat the wine, nutmeg, and minced garlic to a simmer. Add the cheeses, reduce the heat to medium-low, and vigorously whisk or stir with a wooden spoon until all the cheese is melted.

With a fork, mix the flour into the Kirsch until blended then pour into the cheese mixture and mix well. If the cheese mixture has become too thick, add a little wine and blend in. With a rubber spatula, scrape the melted cheese mixture into the fondue pot. Keep the flame on low and serve with fondue forks and cubes of bread for dunking.

IDEAS AND SUBSTITUTIONS

Ideally, if you can find a white wine from the French Savoie, use it for this dish and for drinking! If not, any dry white wine will do.

BURGUNDY BEEF FONDUE WITH DIPPING SAUCES

La Fondue Bourguignonne SERVES 6

Equally as much fun as a cheese fondue is a beef fondue, a specialty from the Burgundy region of France. Imagine a variety of dipping sauces in bowls on your table, a basket of sliced crusty baguette, good Dijon mustard, some small boiled potatoes or fingerlings, and a bubbling pot of hot oil in the center where each person dips in pieces of beef to quickly cook before bringing them back to their plates.

You can serve as many dipping sauces in serving bowls on the table as you wish. Here are recipes for three sauces to get you started!

SPECIAL EQUIPMENT LARGE SAUCEPAN; LARGE FONDUE POT WITH FLAME OR DEEP CHAFING DISH WITH FLAME OR DEEP ELECTRIC SKILLET; INSTANT-READ THERMOMETER; FONDUE FORKS OR CHOPSTICKS; HAND-HELD ELECTRIC MIXER

2 cups (480 ml) canola or grapeseed oil	3 pounds (1.350 kg) beef tenderloin, room temperature	1 jar cornichons or tiny dill pickles
2 cups (480 ml) olive oil	1 long French baguette	

PREP

Slice beef into 1-inch (2.5 cm) cubes.

COOK

Heat the oils in the saucepan over medium heat then transfer to the fondue pot. The thermometer should read somewhere between 350–375° F (180–190° C).

Everyone will spear cubes of beef and cook them in the hot oil then dip them into the sauces they have spooned onto their plates. Serve with slices of warm baguette and cornichons.

RÉMOULADE SAUCE

1 cup (225 g) mayonnaise	2 teaspoons chopped capers	1/2 teaspoon chopped fresh or dried tarragon
1 tablespoon dill relish	1 teaspoon Dijon mustard	

COOK

Mix the above ingredients well and spoon into a serving bowl.

AÏOLI SAUCE

2 egg yolks, room temperature

½ teaspoon Dijon mustard

⅛ teaspoon salt

1 cup (240 ml) extra virgin
   olive oil

6 cloves garlic

COOK

With the mixer, beat the egg yolks, mustard, and salt for 1 minute. Slowly drip in the olive oil while beating until the sauce thickens to a mayonnaise consistency. Finely mince the garlic and stir in. Spoon into a serving bowl.

BLUE CHEESE SAUCE

1½ cups (360 ml) half-and-half
   or heavy cream

4 ounces (110 g) Roquefort
   cheese, crumbled

4 cracks coarsely ground black
   pepper

1 clove garlic, minced

COOK

Bring the half-and-half to a boil, add the cheese, and whisk well to blend. Reduce to a simmer and whisk until the cheese is melted and the sauce is smooth. Season with pepper and garlic and pour into a serving bowl.

IDEAS AND SUBSTITUTIONS

I've also been intrigued with the idea of, instead of the traditional oil, using Burgundy wine to cook the meat. Sounds delicious, doesn't it?

SLOW-COOKER BEANS, DUCK, PORK, CHICKEN, AND SAUSAGE STEW

Le Cassoulet SERVES 4–6

Of all of the recipes in French cuisine, cassoulet—a sumptuous casserole of beans, various meats, and sausages—is tailor-made for a slow cooker because of its lengthy cooking time.

This specialty from Gascony and the Languedoc region in the south of France is a peasant dish that each town has their own way of making. Some use duck confit, some have a breadcrumb topping, some do not. If I can find or make duck confit, I add it, because it enhances the flavor of the stew. If not, I do what most people do in France, which is to use whatever flavorful meats are at hand. Feel free to mix it up, using a variety of sausages, perhaps a smoked ham hock, lamb, or pork ribs.

Cassoulet is one of those dependable dishes that can be made ahead and reheated. It can feed a lot of people, and is excellent as a leftover.

SPECIAL EQUIPMENT LARGE SKILLET; 6 ½-QUART (6-L) SLOW COOKER

3 duck breasts

8 sausages, garlic or kielbasa, smoked, sweet Italian, or fennel

½ pound (225 g) thick-cut bacon, sliced into ½-inch (1.5 cm) pieces

salt and coarsely ground black pepper, to taste

olive oil to brown meats

4 boneless chicken thighs, skin on

1 pound (450 g) boneless pork shoulder, sliced into 1-inch (2.5 cm) pieces

6 cloves garlic, peeled and sliced

1½ tablespoons herbes de Provence

1 large onion, peeled and sliced

3 medium carrots, peeled and cut into 1-inch (2.5-cm) pieces

1 (6-ounce / 170-g) can tomato paste

3 cups (720 ml) dry white wine or chicken stock

4 (15-ounce / 420-g) cans cannellini beans

PREP

Slice slits in the fat layer of the duck breasts then slice each breast into ½-inch (1.5-cm) pieces. Slice each sausage into 3 pieces.

COOK

Cook the bacon in the skillet until crisp and toss into the slow cooker, adding a tablespoon of bacon fat as well. Wipe out the skillet with a paper towel.

Liberally salt and pepper the duck. Add a tablespoon of olive oil to the skillet and brown the duck.

Toss into the slow cooker including any duck fat and bits from the bottom of the skillet.

Liberally salt and pepper the chicken, add a little oil, brown in the skillet, and toss in the slow cooker, including any bits or juices from the bottom of the skillet.

Liberally salt and pepper the pork, add a little oil, brown, and toss in the slow cooker with any juices from the bottom of the skillet. Brown the sausages and toss into the slow cooker.

To the slow cooker, add the garlic, herbes de Provence, onion, carrots, tomato paste, wine, and cannellini beans and stir to mix. Give a final sprinkle of salt and a liberal grinding of black pepper.

Cover and cook on high for 4 hours. Take the cover off the slow cooker and place it at an angle over the top to allow evaporation, and cook another 30 minutes. Allow the cassoulet to rest for 20 minutes before serving.

IDEAS AND SUBSTITUTIONS

Dartagnan.com is my source for duck and armagnac sausages, dried French Coco Tarbais beans from southwest France, duck confit legs to add more flavor to the cassoulet, duck fat, and garlic sausage. With these superior ingredients, you can achieve a cassoulet that has full-bodied flavor and texture comparable to one you would be served in southwest France.

Keep the cassoulet in the refrigerator for a day or two before serving if you want to make it ahead because it tastes better the longer it sits. Serve with a red wine, a light green salad, and slices of thick country bread which I like to baste with olive oil and garlic and warm in the oven before placing on the table.

For a crispy topping, transfer the cassoulet to an oven-proof casserole and finish off by showering with Panko breadcrumbs you have whizzed in a food processor to break down, bits of butter, and baking at 400° F (200 ° C) until golden brown and crisp on top. If you like, serve it with grated cheese, as they do in the city of Toulouse.

LAYERED VEGETABLE OMELET CAKE

Le Crespéou SERVES 6

The open-air market in Saint-Tropez in the south of France has a vendor who makes a savory "cake" made from vegetable omelets that are stacked. Her omelets are thick, the cake is quite high yet compact, and she sells it in wedges. It's divine. I've also seen this dish made with very thin delicate omelets, not very high, circled by a tomato sauce.

Le Crespéou is a dish made in Provence and in the higher villages in the Alpes-de-Haute-Provence. The word crespéou means that the omelet cake looks like it is made with crepes. It's not hard to make and it creates a stunning presentation, easily serving 6.

Make it the day before you want to serve it, wrap it in aluminum foil, and refrigerate. The following are recipes for the layers of the cake and for the sauce to serve with it once it is at room temperature. Stack the layers as you make them, and make as few or as many as you wish depending on how high you would like your cake.

SPECIAL EQUIPMENT BOX GRATER; 9-INCH (23-CM) NONSTICK SKILLET; 9-INCH (23-CM) SPRINGFORM PAN; OLIVE OIL NONSTICK COOKING SPRAY; LARGE PLATE TO FIT OVER SKILLET; ALUMINUM FOIL; LARGE SERVING PLATE OR CAKE STAND; FOOD PROCESSOR

Green Omelet

1 medium zucchini (about 7 heaping tablespoons grated)

1 clove garlic

1 teaspoon fresh thyme leaves or dried

4 large eggs, room temperature

1 tablespoon (15 ml) water (or cream or half-and-half)

salt and freshly ground black pepper, to taste

1 tablespoon (15 ml) extra virgin olive oil for the skillet

Red Omelet

1 large red bell pepper (about 6 heaping tablespoons grated)

4 large eggs, room temperature

1 tablespoon (15 ml) water (or cream or half-and-half)

salt and freshly ground black pepper, to taste

dash of cayenne pepper

1 tablespoon (15 ml) extra virgin olive oil for the skillet

Yellow Omelet

1 medium yellow zucchini (about 6 heaping tablespoons grated)

1 clove garlic

4 large eggs, room temperature

1 tablespoon (15 ml) water (or cream or half-and-half)

salt and freshly ground black pepper, to taste

1 tablespoon (15 ml) extra virgin olive oil for the skillet

Green Pea and Carrot Omelet

½ small onion

2 tablespoons (30 ml) extra virgin olive oil, divided

½ teaspoon sugar

1 clove garlic, peeled and minced

4 large eggs, room temperature

1 tablespoon (15 ml) water (or cream or half-and-half)

salt and freshly ground black pepper, to taste

¼ teaspoon ground turmeric

¼ cup (25 g) freshly grated Parmesan cheese

¾ cup (100 g) frozen peas and carrots, thawed

continued >

PREP FOR GREEN OMELET

Grate the zucchini on the big holes of the box grater and squeeze dry in a paper towel. Peel and mince the garlic. Toss the zucchini, garlic, and thyme together. Whisk the eggs with the water, salt, and pepper, and then stir in the zucchini mixture. Make the omelet as instructed below and place in the springform pan.

PREP FOR RED OMELET

Grate the bell pepper on the big holes of the box grater and squeeze dry in a paper towel. Whisk the eggs with the water, salt, pepper, and cayenne then stir in the bell pepper. Make the omelet as instructed below. If an omelet is already in the springform pan, spread it with the cheese mixture then place this omelet on top and press down.

PREP FOR YELLOW OMELET

Grate the zucchini on the big holes of the box grater and squeeze dry in a paper towel. Peel and mince the garlic and add to the zucchini. Whisk the eggs with the water, salt, and pepper, and then stir in the zucchini mixture. Make the omelet as instructed below and place in the springform pan. If an omelet is already in the springform pan, spread it with the cheese mixture then place this omelet on top and press down.

PREP FOR GREEN PEA AND CARROT OMELET

Slice the onion very thinly and cook in 1 tablespoon olive oil in the skillet until almost golden. Add the sugar, turn up the heat, and cook until caramelized and light brown. Add the garlic and cook for 1 minute. Whisk the eggs together with water, salt, pepper, and turmeric then stir in the Parmesan cheese and peas and carrots. Make the omelet as instructed below. If an omelet is already in the springform pan, spread it with the cheese mixture then place this one on top.

COOK

Spray the springform pan with nonstick cooking spray.

Heat olive oil in the skillet then pour an omelet mixture into the skillet, making sure to completely coat the bottom. Cook on medium-low heat, without stirring and with a cover on, until the bottom of the egg mixture is set and slightly golden, about 2 minutes. Cover the skillet with a large plate, invert the skillet so the omelet is on the plate, then slip the omelet back into the skillet to barely cook the other side. Transfer to the springform pan.

Repeat this process for each color of omelet, for as many omelets as you wish to make, alternating colors as you stack them. Between each omelet layer, lightly spread the cheese mixture that will act like glue to hold them together. Try to select one that looks the best for the first layer, which when inverted will be the top of your "cake."

After you have finished your last omelet, press it down with your fingers. If there is space between the omelets and the edges of the springform pan, crumple aluminum foil and fit in the void all the way around. Then lay plastic wrap over the top and wrap the entire springform pan with foil. Place a weight on top and refrigerate overnight. The weight will help to compress the cake and make it easier to hold together when slicing.

The next day, invert onto the serving plate and serve with the sauce.

CHEESE SPREAD

| 2 (8-ounce / 225–g) packages cream cheese, softened | enough milk to make a spreadable paste | 1 teaspoon herbes de Provence |

COOK

In a bowl, mash or beat the cream cheese with the milk and herbes de Provence until you have a spreadable paste. If needed, warm in microwave for 30 seconds to make more spreadable. Use this to spread over each omelet layer.

SAUCE

4 sun-dried tomatoes

2 cloves garlic, peeled and sliced

1 1/2 teaspoons sugar

1 teaspoon red wine vinegar

2 medium red bell peppers, seeded and coarsely chopped

3 Roma tomatoes, sliced

3 tablespoons extra virgin olive oil

salt and freshly ground black pepper, to taste

COOK

In the bowl of the food processor, add all of the ingredients and process until it reaches the consistency of a sauce, adding a little water, if needed, to thin to your liking. Taste for seasoning and adjust. Pulse to blend then serve with the crespéou.

IDEAS AND SUBSTITUTIONS

You can be totally creative with your fillings. Try whole asparagus spears you have sliced very thin vertically then chopped, chopped fresh spinach, tomatoes, julienned basil leaves, goat cheese, grated cheese, mushrooms, sliced green or black olives, tapenade, minced artichoke hearts, anchovies, eggplant, cooked salmon with capers, or any leftover roasted vegetables. It's a great way of using up what you have on hand.

If you prefer making crepes, the same technique can be used to create a towering cake. If you want to make thinner egg omelets, use just use two eggs per omelet.

SEA SCALLOPS WITH SAUVIGNON BLANC SABAYON

Coquilles Saint-Jacques en Sabayon au Sauvignon Blanc SERVES 4

The frothy whipped egg yolk sauce called zabaglione *in Italy is referred to as* sabayon *in France. The Italian version originated in the Piedmont region of Italy and traveled to France when Catherine de' Medici brought her chefs with her when she married King Henry II. Although most frequently appearing on menus as a sweet sauce or dessert, it is also made in a savory version and served with fish or vegetables.*

I love spooning a golden cloud of it over sautéed scallops. The combination of the light-as-air sauce over hot and crispy scallops works beautifully. You can dress it up with a scattering of caviar on top or dress it down with a side of simply tossed greens.

SPECIAL EQUIPMENT SMALL SAUCEPAN; DOUBLE BOILER WITH LID, OR A LARGE HEATPROOF BOWL OVER A POT OF HOT WATER; HAND-HELD ELECTRIC MIXER; LARGE NONSTICK SKILLET; 4 DINNER PLATES

1 ½ organic lemons

1 sprig fresh tarragon or ¼ teaspoon dried

⅔ cup (160 ml) Sauvignon Blanc wine

2 medium shallots, peeled and minced

¼ teaspoon kosher salt

⅛ teaspoon white pepper

pinch of sugar

5 large egg yolks, room temperature

¼ cup (½ stick / 60 g) unsalted butter, softened

4 tablespoons (60 ml) extra virgin olive oil

12 large sea scallops

PREP

Juice the ½ lemon and slice the whole lemon into quarters. Pull the tarragon leaves from the stems and coarsely chop the leaves. Discard the stems.

COOK

Sabayon Sauce

In the saucepan, bring the wine, 1 teaspoon lemon juice, tarragon, shallots, salt, pepper, and sugar to a boil then reduce the heat to a simmer and cook for about 3 minutes. Strain into a bowl and reserve.

In the double boiler over simmering water, beat the egg yolks constantly with the mixer until pale yellow, thick, and fluffy. Turn the heat to low and very slowly whisk in the wine mixture, bit by bit, until the sauce is thickened. Keep whisking over low heat, but do not allow to boil. When thick, remove from the heat, add the butter, and whisk to completely blend. Taste to see if you need salt and

pepper. Remove from the heat and partially cover to keep warm.

Scallops

In the skillet, heat the olive oil over medium-high heat. When shimmering hot, sear the scallops on one side without moving, until brown, about 2 minutes. Turn over and sear the other side, until they are opaque in the center and golden brown, about 1–2 minutes.

Divide the scallops between the plates, spoon the Sabayon Sauce over the top and side with a quarter of lemon.

IDEAS AND SUBSTITUTIONS

Try making the sabayon with sparkling wine or Champagne, spoon over oysters, and run them under the broiler until lightly golden.

If you use smaller or fewer scallops, this dish makes an ideal appetizer as well.

Boucherie

Charcuterie

Artisanale

de

Père en Fils

THICK GRILLED STEAKS WITH PEPPERCORNS AND COGNAC SAUCE

Steaks au Poivre SERVES 4

This is one of the first dishes I think of making on a special occasion, especially if I have a great bottle of red wine to go with it. If you use the best-quality thick steaks you can find, it becomes one of the most satisfying steak dishes you'll ever make. Served with thin French fries or aligot *mashed potatoes, it is a quick, easy, and absolutely delicious meal.*

SPECIAL EQUIPMENT SMALL FOOD PROCESSOR OR MORTAR AND PESTLE; 1 OR 2 LARGE SKILLETS (DEPENDING ON THE SIZE OF YOUR STEAKS); INSTANT-READ OR MEAT THERMOMETER; ALUMINUM FOIL; SMALL SAUCEPAN; 4 DINNER PLATES

4 tablespoons peppercorns (a mix of dried black and green)

sea salt or kosher salt, to taste

4 (1 to 2-inch / 2.5 to 5-cm) thick rib-eye or Delmonico steaks, room temperature

4 tablespoons (60 ml) extra virgin olive oil

2 tablespoons (30 g) unsalted butter

3 medium shallots, peeled and minced

4 tablespoons (60 ml) cognac, divided

½ cup (120 ml) beef broth

¾ cup (180 ml) heavy cream

PREP

Coarsely crush the peppercorns in a small food processor.

COOK

Salt the steaks on both sides. Using your fingers, press a fourth of the crushed peppercorns firmly onto each of the steaks, on one side only, to make a crust.

Heat the oil in the skillet until it is shimmering hot. Place the steaks in the skillet, non-peppercorn side first, and cook without moving for 4–5 minutes then turn over and cook the other side until the thermometer reads 110–115° F (44–46° C). Transfer to a plate to rest while you make the sauce, loosely tenting steaks with aluminum foil.

Into the skillet, add the butter and shallots and cook for 2 minutes, scraping the bottom of the skillet with a wooden spoon to bring up the bits on the bottom.

In the saucepan, heat 3 tablespoons (45 ml) cognac, remove from the heat, and ignite. When the flames have died, pour the cognac and broth into the skillet, add the cream, and whisk all together. Simmer for 3 minutes then add the remaining cognac and whisk.

Place one steak on each plate and ladle the sauce over the top and around the sides.

IDEAS AND SUGGESTIONS

Try a mixture of all sorts of peppercorns, black, white, green, and pink. If you have brandy and not cognac, use it, or a nice red wine. Some sautéed mushrooms added to the sauce is also quite good.

ALSATIAN SAUERKRAUT AND MEATS PLATTER

Le Choucroute Garnie SERVES 4

Choucroute garnie is a family feast, or feast for a crowd, meant to be placed in the center of the table for all to share.

When in Paris, I head over to Brasserie Bofinger, the Alsatian brasserie near the Bastille, founded in 1864, for their choucroute garnie. I settle in for an hour or more, and if I am on my own, it becomes a feast for one. They serve theirs on a bed of sauerkraut which is tender and mellow from being cooked in white wine and pork. It is piled onto a large serving platter, sided with ovals of steamed potatoes, and topped with frankfurters and smoked meats. There's also a pot of mustard and slices of dark dense bread to go with it. Give me a rainy cold day in Paris and my choucroute garnie and I am happy!

This recipe significantly pares down the normal preparation time for the dish by eliminating a few steps, but the resulting meal is, for me, equally satisfying and quick enough to prepare that I can get it to the table within 30–40 minutes.

SPECIAL EQUIPMENT SMALL FOOD PROCESSOR OR MORTAR AND PESTLE; 3 LARGE SAUCEPANS; LARGE SERVING PLATTER

- 8 juniper berries
- 1 small handful curly parsley
- 8 small to medium Yukon gold potatoes, peeled
- 2 pounds (900 g) sauerkraut
- 3 cups (720 ml) dry white wine, Alsatian white wine or dry Riesling, if possible

- 2 bay leaves
- 8 whole black peppercorns
- 4 thick, smoked pork chops or 4 regular pork chops
- 4 good-quality bratwurst (veal, beef, or pork sausage)
- 4 good-quality weisswurst (white veal and pork sausage)

- 4 skinless good-quality frankfurters
- whole-grain mustard and bread

PREP

Crush the juniper berries in the small food processor. Pull the parsley leaves off the stems and finely chop. Discard the stems.

COOK

Cook the potatoes in a saucepan of simmering salted water until fork tender, about 20–30 minutes.

Place the sauerkraut, wine, bay leaves, crushed juniper berries, and peppercorns in a saucepan and simmer for 30 minutes (check the instructions on the package of sauerkraut to determine how long to cook it, as it may vary). If the pork chops are smoked then add them to this saucepan and cook along with the sauerkraut. At the end of cooking, remove the bay leaves and discard.

If the pork chops are not smoked or precooked, simmer them in a skillet of water with a lid on until they are cooked through and no longer pink inside.

Time will vary depending on the thickness of the pork chops.

Simmer the bratwurst, weisswurst, and frankfurters in water in a saucepan until fully warmed through.

Mound the sauerkraut and its juices down the center of the warmed serving platter then arrange the meats and boiled potatoes over the top, scatter the parsley over the potatoes, and place the platter in the center of the table with mustard, bread, and a pepper mill. Cold beer or a chilled Alsatian or Riesling wine would be the perfect accompaniment.

IDEAS AND SUBSTITUTIONS

If you can find large cans or bottles of sauerkraut already cooked in white wine or Champagne, you can eliminate the step of cooking the sauerkraut in white wine and just warm it in a saucepan.

FRESH MUSSELS IN WHITE WINE

Moules à la Marinière SERVES 4

Fabulous with French fries, this drool-worthy dish is simple and quick to make. So quick, in fact, that you should make the French fries ahead and keep them warm in the oven while the mussels cook. Also place a baguette to warm in the oven to be ready to use to sop up the broth.

I first experienced this dish in Trouville, in Normandy, at a restaurant where they added a final splash of cream before serving. Each and every mouthful of the wine-soaked bread that had been dragged through the remaining sauce at the end of the meal was a wonder.

SPECIAL EQUIPMENT VERY LARGE POT WITH LID; 4 SHALLOW SOUP BOWLS; LARGE BOWL

- 4 to 5 pounds (1.8 to 2.2 kg) fresh mussels
- 1 small handful flat-leaf parsley
- 2 sprigs fresh tarragon
- 3 tablespoons (45 ml) extra virgin olive oil
- 4 cloves garlic, peeled and finely chopped
- 3 large shallots, peeled and finely chopped
- 3 to 4 cups (720 ml to 1 l) Muscadet wine or other dry white wine
- salt and freshly ground white pepper, to taste
- ¼ cup (60 ml) dry white vermouth
- 1 long French baguette, sliced

PREP

Clean the mussels by scrubbing them with a brush under cold running water. Pull off the beards and throw away any that are open. Keep them in cold water until you are ready to use.

Pull the leaves off the parsley and tarragon stems and finely chop. Discard stems.

COOK

In the pot, heat the olive oil, add the garlic and shallots, and cook on medium for 2 minutes. Add the wine, tarragon, a little salt and pepper, and bring to a boil. Drop in all the mussels, cover with the lid, and cook on medium for a couple of minutes, shaking the pot once or twice. Pick up the lid and peek inside. If all the mussels have opened, the dish is ready. Throw away any mussels that are still closed.

With a slotted spoon, scoop up the mussels and divide between the soup bowls. Whisk the vermouth into the sauce then equally ladle over the tops of the mussels. Sprinkle with the chopped parsley and serve immediately. Place the large bowl on the table for the shells and have a basket of sliced baguette nearby to sop up the delicious sauce at the bottom of the bowls.

IDEAS AND SUGGESTIONS

I love adding a tablespoon of Pernod to the white wine for a hint of anise. A richer dish can be made by taking the mussels out and whisking in a mixture of ¼ cup (60 ml) cream and 2 egg yolks until the sauce thickens a little then pour it all over the mussels.

For a casual dinner, make some French fries and pile them in the center of the table on a large piece of wax paper with salt within reach. They are the traditional accompaniment to Moules à la Marinière.

DUCK BREASTS WITH BLACK CHERRY SAUCE

Magret de Canard Montmorency SERVES 4

The village of Montmorency is located just north of Paris and was once famous for its Montmorency cherry orchards, which are now mostly gone. However, this dish is still made there to celebrate the slightly sour cherry. I had it several years ago in a small restaurant on the road to Montmorency, where it was served as a whole roast duck with a ruby-red sauce.

I make mine with duck breasts and use fresh cherries when they are available and Montmorency cherries if I can find them. Otherwise, frozen, canned, or bottled dark sour cherries are fine. The tart cherry sauce balances the rich flavor of the duck for a truly addictive combination and is an old-world recipe rarely found on menus anymore that can be made at home in a flash.

SPECIAL EQUIPMENT NONSTICK SKILLET; INSTANT-READ THERMOMETER; SAUCEPAN

- 4 Magret duck breasts, room temperature
- 12 ounces (340 g) frozen, canned, or bottled sour dark cherries (Montmorency, if possible)
- kosher salt and freshly ground black pepper, to taste
- 2 medium shallots, peeled and minced
- 2 cups (480 ml) dry red wine
- 1/2 cup (120 ml) cherry jam or preserves
- 1/4 teaspoon ground cinnamon
- 2 tablespoons (16 g) sugar
- 1 medium organic orange, zested and juiced
- 4 tablespoons (30 g) flour

PREP

Slice slits in the duck fat layer to create a criss-cross pattern, slicing all the way down to the meat layer, but not cutting into the meat. If using frozen cherries, thaw them in a bowl of warm water then pat dry.

COOK

Duck

Generously salt and pepper the duck breasts, place them fat side down in a hot skillet, and cook over low heat for about 10 minutes, until you see the fat has turned into liquid and what is left on the duck is crispy and golden brown. Pour off most of the fat and reserve. Turn the breasts over so the fat side is up and cook for another 8 minutes. Check with the instant-read thermometer, and when it reaches 135° F (58° C), remove the breasts to a cutting board and allow them to rest. You don't want to overcook duck. It should be pink inside.

Sauce

Pour 2 tablespoons of the reserved duck fat into the saucepan and cook the shallots over medium heat for 2 minutes. Add the wine, jam, cinnamon, sugar, orange zest, and orange juice and bring to a simmer. Take 1/2 cup (120 ml) of the sauce and mix it with the flour then pour back into the saucepan and vigorously whisk while it comes back to a simmer. Cook until the sauce is thickened. Add the cherries and cook until they are warmed through.

Thinly slice the breasts and divide between serving plates. Ladle the sauce and cherries alongside the breasts.

IDEAS AND SUBSTITUTIONS

Save any remaining duck fat. It's one of the healthiest animal fats and has great flavor. It can be kept covered in the refrigerator for a few days and used as you would any oil.

BISTRO FLANK STEAK WITH PORT SAUCE

Bavette du Bistrot, Sauce au Porto SERVES 4

French fast food at its finest, this bistro dish is normally served with French fries and salad. Marinate the steaks overnight and simply grill them the next day, making a quick pan sauce to ladle over them. Flank steak is an inexpensive cut of meat usually accompanied with a shallot or blue cheese or port sauce, and makes a rapid yet elegant weeknight meal.

SPECIAL EQUIPMENT LARGE SEALABLE PLASTIC BAG; BARBECUE GRILL OR STOVE TOP GRILL PAN; SMALL SAUCEPAN

¾ cup (180 ml) port, divided

2 tablespoons (30 ml) balsamic vinegar

¼ cup (45 g) dark brown sugar

2 cloves garlic, peeled and minced

2 shallots, peeled and thinly sliced

1 tablespoon Dijon mustard

¼ teaspoon salt

¼ teaspoon freshly ground black pepper

½ teaspoon dried thyme

2 pounds (900 g) flank steak

1 tablespoon (15g) unsalted butter

COOK

In a bowl, add ½ cup (120 ml) port, vinegar, brown sugar, garlic, shallots, mustard, salt, pepper, and thyme to make a marinade. Whisk well to combine and pour into the plastic bag. Add the steak, seal the bag, toss to coat the steak with the marinade, and refrigerate overnight or for at least 5 hours. Remove the steak and reserve the marinade.

Bring the steak to room temperature before grilling. Preheat grill until very hot. Salt and pepper the steak and grill to the desired degree of doneness, usually 2–3 minutes per side for medium rare. Allow to rest for 5 minutes then thinly slice the steak against the grain and divide between serving plates.

In the saucepan, bring the reserved marinade to a boil, add remaining port, and simmer for 1 minute. Whisk in the butter until the sauce is glossy then pour over slices of steak and serve.

IDEAS AND SUBSTITUTIONS

If you substitute dry red wine for the port, you will be making a sauce à la Bordelaise.

CHARCUTERIE

JAMBON SEC
SAUCISSON SEC
ANDOUILLETTES - BO
CAILLETTES - RILLET
PATÉ DE CAMPAGNE
TRIPES A LA PROVEN
MERGUEZ-CHIPOLA
SAUCISSES-FIGATELL
MORTADELLE-SALAMI-CO

VIANDES DE BŒUF
ORIGINE FRANÇE

AGNEAUX DE PAYS

VOLAILLES FERMIÈRES

VIANDES DE PORC
ET DE VEAU

SPÉCIALITÉS
MAISON
PATÉ DE CAMPAGNE
PIEDS — PAQUETS
RILLONS AUX HERBES
BOUDIN NOIR
CAILLETTES

GASCONY ROAST LEG OF LAMB WITH ANCHOVIES AND GARLIC

Gigot d'agneau en Gasconnade, avec de l'Ail et des Anchois SERVES 4–6

I had the pleasure a few years ago of spending a day in the kitchen of Pierre Koffmann, the celebrated 3 Michelin-star chef at La Tante Claire in London, watching him cook. As I was leaving, he handed me a signed copy of his cookbook, Memories of Gascony. His stories, recipes, and obvious love for Gascony and its style of cooking, won me over and I faithfully tried making most of the recipes in the book as they were homey and approachable. As he walked me to the door that day, he told me about the way they roast a leg of lamb in Gascony, with anchovies and garlic. It has become my favorite way to make lamb, and the only change I ever make is to sometimes add rosemary leaves.

SPECIAL EQUIPMENT LARGE SKILLET; ROASTING PAN WITH ROASTING RACK; MEAT THERMOMETER

1 (4 to 5-pound / 1.8 to 2.2-kg) bone-in leg of lamb

2 sprigs fresh thyme

2 (2-ounce / 60-g) cans anchovies in oil

12 large cloves garlic, peeled and sliced in half vertically

salt, to taste

coarsely ground black pepper, to taste

7 tablespoons (105 ml) extra virgin olive oil, divided

6 russet potatoes, cut into quarters

6 large carrots, sliced into 1-inch pieces

3 medium yellow onions, peeled and sliced in half

2 cups (480 ml) dry red wine

1 tablespoon (8 g) all-purpose flour

PREP

Preheat oven to 450° F (230° C).

Wash and pat dry the lamb. Pull the leaves off the sprigs of thyme and discard the stems. Take the anchovies out of their cans, reserving 2 for the sauce.

COOK

Lamb

With a small sharp knife, make slits all over the leg of lamb and insert garlic halves. Reserve any leftover garlic for tossing into the bottom of the roasting pan.

Continue in the same manner by making slits and inserting one anchovy per slit. Generously coat the entire lamb with salt and pepper.

In the skillet, heat 3 tablespoons (45 ml) olive oil until it shimmers then brown the lamb on all sides. Pour remaining olive oil in the bottom of the roasting pan; add the potatoes, carrots, onions, garlic, and thyme leaves then toss around to coat. Place the leg of lamb on the roasting rack, and roast at 450° F (230° C) for 15 minutes.

Turn the oven temperature down to 350° F (180° C) and roast for another 35–45 minutes, or until the thermometer reads 130° F (55° C) for rare or 145° F (63° C) for medium-rare. Allow the lamb to rest on a cutting board for 10 minutes then slice across the grain and arrange on a serving platter with the vegetables from the roasting pan.

Sauce

Deglaze the roasting pan by adding the red wine whisked with the flour. Place the pan on the stove over medium heat, and with a wooden spoon, stir up any browned bits at the bottom of the pan. Mash in the reserved anchovies, bring to a simmer, whisk well, and then simmer for 2 minutes. Pour into a serving pitcher and place on the table with the platter of sliced lamb.

IDEAS AND SUGGESTIONS

Serve with a full-bodied red or white Burgundy and a great salad.

GRANDMOTHER'S CHICKEN

Poulet Grand-Mère SERVES 4

Grandmother's Chicken is an all-in-one-pot kind of dish that is garnished with a scattering of crisp pieces of potato and bacon. It is full of flavor and hits a note that is deeply comforting. I like serving this over egg noodles.

SPECIAL EQUIPMENT LARGE SKILLET; DUTCH OVEN

8 chicken thighs, skin on

all-purpose flour for dredging

salt and coarsely ground black or white pepper, to taste

4 sprigs fresh thyme or 2 teaspoons dried thyme

2 medium Yukon gold potatoes, peeled and cut into ¼-inch (6-mm) cubes

3 tablespoons (45 ml) extra virgin olive oil

3 cups (720 ml) dry white wine

2 tablespoons (30 g) tomato paste

2 teaspoons red currant jelly

16 button mushrooms, sliced in half

½ pound (225 g) bacon, sliced into thin matchsticks

4 cloves garlic, peeled and minced

3 medium shallots, peeled and minced

½ pound (225 g) boiled ham, sliced into ¼-inch (6-mm) cubes

cooked egg noodles

PREP

Rinse and pat dry chicken. Place flour on a plate and liberally season with salt and pepper. Pull leaves off thyme sprigs. Discard sprigs. Place the potatoes in a bowl of cold water until ready to use.

COOK

In the skillet over medium-high heat, add the oil and heat until shimmering. Liberally season the chicken with salt and pepper, lightly dredge in the seasoned flour, and place in the skillet to brown—about 8 minutes on the skin side then 4 minutes on the other side.

To the Dutch oven, add the wine, tomato paste, thyme, and jelly; whisk and bring to boil. Reduce to a gentle simmer. Add the cooked chicken and mushrooms and cook for 15 minutes.

Meanwhile, wipe out the skillet and cook the bacon until browned and crisp. Remove to paper towels and set aside. Pat the potatoes dry and cook in the bacon fat until golden brown and crisp. Remove to paper towels.

To the skillet of bacon fat, add the garlic, shallots, and ham and cook 3 minutes. Transfer to the Dutch oven and stir.

Divide the chicken between plates over noodles, pour the sauce around the chicken, and scatter the grand-mère crispy garnishes of potatoes and bacon over the top.

IDEAS AND SUGGESTIONS

Crisply fried pearl onions make a good garnish as well.

OVER-THE-TOP LOBSTER THERMIDOR

Homard Thermidor SERVES 4

Old school and hardly seen anymore on menus, Lobster Thermidor is a feast for a special occasion. It was first created by Marie's Restaurant in Paris, in 1894, to celebrate the opening of the play Thermidor *by Victorien Sardou.*

Imagine a lobster stuffed with lobster meat, cream, and wine then run under the broiler with a grated cheese topping and served bubbly hot and browned.

This is an easy-to-prepare recipe to pull out for birthdays, holidays, celebrations, New Year's Eve, or those days when nothing else will make you happy.

SPECIAL EQUIPMENT LARGE POT BIG ENOUGH TO BOIL LOBSTERS, ONE BY ONE; SAUCEPAN; GRILL PAN TO GO UNDER BROILER

4 sprigs fresh tarragon or 2 teaspoons dried tarragon

2 (2 to 3-pound / 900 g to 1.350-kg) lobsters

4 tablespoons extra virgin olive oil

1 large shallot, peeled and minced

3 tablespoons (25 g) all-purpose flour

½ cup (120 ml) dry white wine

¼ cup (60 ml) sherry

½ cup (120 ml) fat-free half-and-half

¼ teaspoon freshly grated nutmeg

1 teaspoon Dijon mustard

½ teaspoon salt

paprika

1 cup (100 g) grated Parmesan or Gruyère cheese

2 large organic lemons, sliced into quarters

PREP

Pull the tarragon leaves off the stems, mince the leaves, and discard the stems.

COOK

Pour enough water in the pot to be able to cover a lobster and bring it to a rolling boil over high heat. Pick up a lobster with tongs, dunk it into the boiling water, head first, and cover the pot to bring it back to a boil quickly. Cook the lobster until it is bright red, about 6 minutes. (Don't worry about undercooking the lobster because it will cook again under the broiler and you don't want tough lobster). Remove

the lobster from the water and drain. Run under cold running water to cool down and stop cooking.

Bring the water back to a rolling boil and repeat with the second lobster. When they are both cooked and cool to the touch, take a sharp knife, and slice them vertically all the way down the middle, through the chest area and down through the tail, careful to catch the green inside juices and any coral into a bowl.

Remove the lobster meat from the tails, cut into cubes, and toss into a large bowl. Remove the claws from the lobsters, crack them, extract their meat, cut into cubes, and toss into the bowl.

Sauce

Add olive oil to the saucepan, and over medium heat, cook the shallot for 2 minutes. Dump in the flour all at once, whisk to mix, and cook for 2 minutes. Slowly add the wine, sherry, and half-and-half, whisking as you add them, and then whisking to totally combine. Keep whisking and cooking the sauce until it turns thick and creamy, about 2 minutes. Add the nutmeg, mustard, salt, and tarragon and mix well. Thin with a bit more wine or the reserved juices and/ or coral from the lobsters, if desired.

Preheat the broiler.

Add the lobster meat to the sauce in the saucepan and heat until the lobster is hot. Lay the lobster shells in the grill pan. Fill the chest cavity and the tails with the lobster mixture then spoon any remaining sauce over them. Sprinkle with paprika and cheese and run under the broiler until they are golden, about 4 minutes. Serve with lemon quarters.

IDEAS AND SUBSTITUTIONS

When lobsters are in season and drop in price, this makes an impressive party or buffet dish. Count on half of lobster per person and arrange all of them on a large serving platter on a bed of dressed salad greens that people can scoop up onto their plate as well.

Spécialité
Création
Maison

Allumettes
aux
Pralines
2,30 €

SWEET DREAMS

━━

While a cheese board served with bread is the way most French families finish dinner during the week, desserts are the preferred ending on weekends and for entertaining. And although there is no reason to make dessert when there are alluring *pâtissiers* on every block, French home cooks can whip up a host of tried and true French classics for their families without making the trip to the pâtissier, especially ones they have put a spin on and made their own.

The following recipe for Banana Tart Tatin is based on one I had at a friend's house in Provence one summer, a twist on the original apple tart Tatin invented accidentally by the sisters Tatin in the 1800s. A luscious chocolate mousse and a silky crème caramel are everyday family favorites that I've included recipes for, as well as some desserts I've discovered on my travels that found a permanent place in my recipe box. Some of them are only found in the region where they are made, such as the Rum-Soaked Almond Cake from Nantes, the original French macarons cookies from the nuns in Nancy, and the cream-topped apple tart Normande from Normandy.

All are ultimate comfort foods, happily consumed with or without a meal! *Bon appétit!*

BANANA TART TATIN

Tarte Tatin à la Banane SERVES 8

A gooey, messy, less-than-perfect looking dessert, Banana Tart Tatin checks all the boxes for being one of the all-time greatest comfort foods. Once you see how easy it is to make, you will want to make it all the time.

I like to make it in a heavy skillet and arrange the bananas in concentric circles, as they naturally curve and conform to a circular form. Serve with a scoop of vanilla ice cream on top so that it begins to melt in luscious cold vanilla streams over the warm tart.

SPECIAL EQUIPMENT ROLLING PIN; OVEN-PROOF HEAVY OR CAST IRON SKILLET; PARCHMENT PAPER

1 sheet frozen puff pastry, thawed

½ cup (100 g) sugar, plus 3 tablespoons (35 g)

5 tablespoons (75 g) salted butter

1½ teaspoons vanilla extract

6 bananas, not too ripe, peeled and sliced in half vertically or sliced in rounds

PREP

Preheat oven to 350° F (180° C).

COOK

Pastry Crust

On a clean, floured work surface, roll out the pastry a bit larger than the size of your skillet then cut the pastry so that it is round and will fit into the pan. Sandwich it between 2 pieces of parchment paper and keep in the refrigerator until ready to use.

Caramel

In the skillet, add the sugar and cook on medium heat without stirring until you see the sugar begin to bubble and melt then swirl the pan a bit to help it liquidize. After a minute or two when it has turned to a light brown color, remove the skillet from the heat and slice in the butter. It will spatter, so be careful it does not touch your skin. Stir with a wooden spoon until the sugar and butter are blended into a smooth caramel sauce. Whisk in the vanilla.

Banana Tart Tatin

Arrange the bananas in the skillet of caramel sauce rounded side down if they have been cut vertically, or simply lay them in if cut in rounds, in circles from the outside inwards until they are all used. Move them around a bit to create a pleasing circular pattern. Place the skillet on medium heat and cook without moving anything for about 4 minutes. Remove from the heat.

Lay the puff pastry over the top of the bananas and tuck it in a little bit under the bananas around the edges. Slice a few small slits in the pastry. Bake for 20–25 minutes, until golden brown. Remove from the oven and, careful not to let any of the hot caramel sauce drip onto your skin, immediately invert onto a serving plate. You might want to wear oven mitts to do this.

IDEAS AND SUBSTITUTIONS

Try scattering some crushed rosemary leaves in the caramel sauce to add an intriguing scent and taste to the tart or scraping a vanilla bean into the sauce for a more pronounced vanilla flavor.

PERFECT CRÈME CARAMEL

La Crème Caramel Parfaite SERVES 8

I have been making this recipe for over 20 years and it always produces a beautifully high crème caramel with a deep mahogany gloss that sits in a puddle of caramel sauce. Refreshingly cool and light in summer, it can be surrounded with a whimsical garland of fresh mixed berries and sprigs of mint. In winter, try encircling it with a wreath of sugar-frosted cranberries.

SPECIAL EQUIPMENT MEDIUM SAUCEPAN; 8-INCH SOUFFLÉ BAKING DISH; ROASTING PAN OR BAKING DISH

1 ³⁄₄ cups (350 g) sugar, divided

6 large eggs, room temperature

2 large egg whites, room temperature

4 cups (960 ml) whole milk, room temperature

¼ teaspoon salt

1 ¹⁄₂ teaspoons vanilla extract

PREP

Preheat oven to 300° F (150 ° C).

COOK

Caramel Sauce

In the saucepan, heat 1 cup (200 g) sugar over medium-low heat. Once the sugar begins to liquefy, stir continuously until smooth and totally melted. Stop stirring and allow the mixture to bubble around the edges, just come to a boil, and turn dark amber. Remove from the heat, and, being very careful not to burn yourself with spattering hot sugar, pour the syrup into the soufflé dish. Swirl it around and tilt to coat the sides of the dish as well. Allow the hot syrup to harden into a beautiful clear amber coating.

Custard

Place the eggs and egg whites into a large bowl and whisk well to combine. Add the milk, remaining sugar, salt, and vanilla and whisk well.

Pour hot water into the roasting pan, place the soufflé dish in the center, pour in the custard all the way to the top, and place the roasting pan on the middle shelf of the oven. Bake for 1 hour and 25 minutes, until brown around the edges and still wiggly in the center.

Remove from the oven, cool to room temperature, then refrigerate for at least 2 hours or preferably overnight. Place a dish over the top of the soufflé dish and invert to unmold, allowing all the caramel sauce to drip out onto the serving dish around the crème caramel.

IDEAS AND SUBSTITUTIONS

Slice into wedges and serve with whipped cream spiked with Grand Marnier for a special treat.

RICE PUDDING EMPRESS STYLE WITH CUSTARD, CANDIED FRUITS, AND KIRSCH

Riz à l'Impératrice SERVES 6

Riz à l'Impératrice *is a vintage French dessert rarely seen on restaurant menus anymore, much less in family homes. Instead, French families dote on* riz au lait, *a simple rice pudding that is deeply satisfying. I love it too, but have always been fascinated with beautiful illustrations of the classic* Riz à l'Impératrice —*a rich rice pudding made with créme anglais, liqueur-soaked candied fruits, and whipped cream—incorporating either egg whites or gelatin to form a pudding firm enough to be shaped in fancy molds. I make it for formal occasions, yet coax it into a homier version by eliminating the need to mold it.*

My creamy rice pudding is also made with créme anglais, Kirsch-soaked candied fruit, and whipped cream. Spooned out of a large serving bowl or heaped into martini glasses, it makes a cool summer treat or can be jazzed up around the end-of-year holidays with eggnog flavors.

SPECIAL EQUIPMENT LARGE SAUCEPAN WITH A LID, SMALL SAUCEPAN; STAND MIXER

Rice

1 cup (130 g) chopped candied fruit

¾ cup (180 ml) Kirsch, divided

1 cup (190 g) white rice

1¾ cups (350 ml) milk, plus more, as needed

1 teaspoon vanilla extract

½ teaspoon almond extract, divided

5 tablespoons (65 g) sugar

Custard

1 cup (240 ml) milk

½ teaspoon vanilla extract

½ teaspoon almond extract

2 tablespoons (30 ml) Kirsch

3 egg yolks

¼ cup (50 g) sugar

1½ cups (360 ml) heavy cream

PREP FOR RICE

Soak candied fruit in ½ cup (120 ml) Kirsch until ready to use, for at least 15 minutes. Rinse rice in a strainer a couple of times under running water.

COOK
Rice

Pour milk, remaining Kirsch, vanilla, almond extract, and sugar into the large saucepan and bring to a boil. Add the rice then turn down to a simmer.

Give it a good stir, put on the lid, and cook for 20–30 minutes or until the rice is soft and creamy. Stir frequently. Add more milk, if needed, as it depends on the type of rice as to how much liquid is required. I often end up adding anywhere from ¼ cup (60 ml) to 1¼ (300 ml) cups or more to keep cooking the rice until it is firm yet tender, with the liquid evaporated. Cool to room temperature. Mix the candied fruit and the Kirsch they were soaking in into the rice mixture.

Custard

In the small saucepan, bring milk, vanilla, almond extract, and Kirsch to a boil then remove from the heat.

In the stand mixer, add the egg yolks and beat for 1 minute. Add the sugar and beat well, until pale yellow. On low speed, beat in half the milk mixture then pour all back into the saucepan, and on low heat, stir with a wooden spoon until the mixture thickens and coats the back of a spoon. Cool to room temperature.

Whip the cream until it holds its shape.

Stir the rice and custard together then fold in the whipped cream until just blended, trying to maintain as much volume as possible. Scoop into one large bowl or individual serving bowls or glasses and chill for at least 3 hours, preferably overnight.

IDEAS AND SUBSTITUTIONS

For end-of-year holidays, substitute rum or brandy for the Kirsch, and add cinnamon and nutmeg for an eggnog flavor. During the warmer months, drizzle a fresh raspberry or fresh cherry purée over the top and serve.

MERINGUE EGGS ON ORANGE CUSTARD SAUCE

Œufs à la Neige au Orange SERVES 4

One hot summer night in the late 1980s, we arrived at the restaurant Lameloise in Chagny, France, where our favorite chef, Jacques Lameloise presided. We were taken into a lounge area and were given huge menus to order from before being shown into the dining room. They also brought us glasses of Champagne and paper thin slices of saucisson, or salami.

After looking over the elaborate dessert selections, I whispered to my husband that I wished I could just have a simple Œufs à la Neige, and he replied that it wasn't likely as it was a "farmhouse dish."

We went into dinner, and after our main course, I ordered a chocolate tasting plate for dessert. After a few moments, Chef Lameloise appeared at my side offering me an overly large soup bowl with a smile, saying, "Your Œufs à la Neige, Madame!" Touched to the core and with tears in my eyes, I thanked him profusely. How did he know?

We never found out. My best guess is that it is the kind of magic that happens in a truly great restaurant, or it was perhaps a passing waiter who heard my lament?

SPECIAL EQUIPMENT LARGE SAUCEPAN; STAND MIXER OR HAND-HELD ELECTRIC MIXER; SMALL SAUCEPAN

Crème Anglaise

8 large egg yolks, room temperature

2 cups (480 ml) milk

1/4 cup (60 ml) heavy cream

1 organic orange, juiced and zested

4 teaspoons (20 ml) pure orange extract

1/8 teaspoon vanilla extract

1 teaspoon all-purpose flour

2 tablespoons (30 ml) water

1/2 cup (100 g) sugar

Meringue Eggs

8 large egg whites, room temperature

1/4 teaspoon cream of tartar

1 vanilla bean, scraped and seeds reserved

8 tablespoons (100 g) sugar

Caramel Drizzle

1 cup (200 g) sugar

1 tablespoon (15 ml) water

PREP

When you separate the eggs into yolks and whites, make sure there is not a speck of yolk in the whites. Fill a large bowl with water and ice cubes.

COOK

Crème Anglaise

Using the large saucepan, pour in the milk, cream, 1/2 cup (120 ml) orange juice, orange extract, and vanilla and bring just to a boil. In a cup, mix together the flour with water and pour into the saucepan of milk. Whisk to combine, bring back to a boil, and then remove from the heat.

Using the mixer, beat the egg yolks for 1 minute. Add the sugar and beat for 30 seconds on medium, until eggs are pale yellow and thick.

Vigorously whisk 1/2 cup (120 ml) of the hot milk mixture into the egg mixture then pour the egg mixture into the saucepan of milk and whisk on low

continued >

heat until the custard thickens and coats the back of a spoon. Do not boil. Remove from the heat and dip the saucepan immediately into the bowl of ice water, stirring the custard until it has stopped cooking. Whisk in 1 tablespoon orange zest.

When cool, pour into individual serving bowls or one large serving bowl, cover with plastic wrap that touches the custard (to prevent a skin forming), and place in the refrigerator to chill until ready to use.

Meringue Eggs

In the bowl of the stand mixer, beat the egg whites with the cream of tartar until soft peaks form. Add in the scraped vanilla seeds and then sprinkle in the sugar, a little at a time while whipping, until the meringue become glossy and very stiff, about 4–9 minutes. You should be able to turn the bowl over and the meringue will not fall out. If you use a hand mixer rather than a stand mixer, the meringue will take longer to beat.

One by one, mound the meringue into egg shapes on a microwave-safe plate and cook on high for 10 seconds, or just until you see them puff up a bit like a soufflé. Repeat until all eggs are done.

When you are ready to serve desert, float the meringue eggs on top of the custard then make the Caramel Drizzle.

Caramel Drizzle

Pour sugar then water into the small saucepan, place over medium-high heat without stirring, and leave it to bubble away until it is melted and turns an amber color. Immediately drizzle the caramel over each dish using a fork to scoop some up and wave back and forth above the meringue eggs, being careful not to let any of the hot syrup drop onto your skin.

IDEAS OR SUBSTITUTIONS

You can make the Crème Anglaise up to 2 days in advance and keep it chilled in the refrigerator.

NO-RAW-EGGS CHOCOLATE ESPRESSO MOUSSE

Mousse Choco-Expresso MAKES 4 CUPS

French families whip up chocolate mousse all the time using raw eggs, but I wanted to develop a recipe that did not use them. I finally came up with one that works beautifully without raw eggs. It is rich and thick and intensely flavored. I love heaping it into an elegant crystal serving bowl to serve family-style, but it is equally impressive chilled in individual espresso cups or parfait glasses with a swirl of whipped cream on top.

SPECIAL EQUIPMENT STAND MIXER; MEDIUM SAUCEPAN

3 large egg yolks, room temperature

¼ cup (50 g) sugar

¼ teaspoon ground cinnamon

1 cup (240 ml) milk

1 tablespoon plus 2 teaspoons instant espresso powder

1 teaspoon vanilla extract

8 ounces (225 g) semisweet chocolate, chopped

1 cup (240 ml) heavy cream or whipping cream, chilled

COOK

In the stand mixer, beat the egg yolks until pale and thick. Add the sugar and cinnamon and beat until well blended.

In the saucepan, heat the milk, espresso powder, and vanilla until it just comes to a boil. Remove from the heat. With the stand mixer running, pour ½ cup (120 ml) of the hot milk into the egg mixture and beat for 10 seconds. Pour everything back into the saucepan, return to low heat, and, with a wooden spoon, continuously stir until the custard thickens and coats the back of the spoon, about 3 minutes.

Remove from the heat, add the chocolate, and vigorously stir until melted.

Whip the cream until stiff peaks form. Fold ½ cup (120 ml) into the custard until well blended, and then fold in the rest, trying to preserve volume. Spoon into bowls, dessert dishes, or glasses and refrigerate for 3 hours before serving.

IDEAS AND SUBSTITUTIONS

Sift some cocoa and espresso powder together to dust over the top for an added layer of intense chocolate flavor.

VERY LEMON TART IN A BUTTER COOKIE CRUST

Tarte au Citron SERVES 8

I can't pass by a bakery in France and not stop to investigate their tarte au citron. Are they large and covered with meringue? Are they small enough for me to devour in two bites? Are they embellished with lavender or grated lime rind, or have they been made in tiny molds and quiver in the center? I've tried them all, in every village and every town I have been in.

The best one I have ever experienced had a crispy butter cookie crust, while the inside was tender and soft and very tart. This is the closest I have come to replicating that gloriously lemony memory.

SPECIAL EQUIPMENT 9-INCH (23-CM) TART PAN WITH REMOVABLE BOTTOM; FOOD PROCESSOR; STAND MIXER; LARGE SAUCEPAN; INSTANT-READ THERMOMETER

Crust

½ cup (1 stick / 120 g) unsalted butter, chilled, plus more for greasing tart pan

¼ cup (50 g) sugar, plus more for preparing tart pan

1¼ cups (150 g) all-purpose flour

¼ teaspoon ground cinnamon

1 teaspoon vanilla extract

2 to 3 tablespoons (30 to 45 ml) cold water

Filling

6 large eggs, room temperature

½ teaspoon vanilla extract

1 cup sugar (200 g) plus 1 tablespoon, plus more if you wish a sweeter tart

3 lemons, juiced

powdered sugar

PREP FOR CRUST

Liberally butter the tart pan, sprinkle with sugar, and shake off excess.

COOK

Crust

In the food processor, add the flour, sugar, cinnamon, vanilla, and butter and process until it looks like coarse meal. With the machine running, add 2 tablespoons water until the dough comes together when you pinch it. If needed, add an extra tablespoon of water with the machine running. Scrape the contents of the bowl into the tart pan and press down with your fingers to make a crust on the bottom and all the way up the sides. Refrigerate for 30 minutes or until firm.

Meanwhile, preheat the oven to 400° F (200° C). Bake the tart crust for 13–14 minutes, or until golden. Remove from the oven and cool to room temperature.

Reduce oven temperature to 300° F (150 ° C).

Filling

In the stand mixer, beat eggs, vanilla, sugar, and 1 cup (240 ml) lemon juice together until well combined. Taste the filling. I like a sour lemon flavor, so if it is too tart for your taste, add more sugar.

Pour into the saucepan and cook over medium heat. Whisk continuously until the mixture thickens, about 140–145° F (60–63° C) on thermometer, anywhere from 6–11 minutes.

Pour the filling into the pastry crust and bake until set, about 15 minutes. Remove from the oven and cool to room temperature. Shake a fine sieve of powdered sugar over the top of the tart before slicing.

IDEAS AND SUGGESTIONS

Many recipes call for butter to be added to the filling, but I like it without. If you would like a richer taste, whisk in 4 tablespoons (60 g) unsalted butter at the end of cooking the filling on the stove and before you pour it into the pastry crust to bake.

Blood oranges instead of lemons will produce a beautiful salmon-colored tart filling. To garnish, top with raspberries or blueberries, or with a beautiful orange dust—peel 2 oranges, shave off white pith, cook peel for 15 minutes in 1 cup (240 ml) water and ½ cup (100 g) sugar, drain, bake at 350° F (180° C) for 15 minutes (do not allow to brown), cool to room temperature, then grind in spice mill and dust the top of the tart.

PROFITEROLES BATHED IN DARK CHOCOLATE SAUCE

Profiteroles Baignées de Sauce au Chocolat Noir MAKES ABOUT 18

Profiteroles are as easy to make as cookies. It's simply a different method, and once you learn the process, it moves along rapidly. You just throw everything into a saucepan, mix well, then spoon mounds of the mixture onto a baking tray and bake. Remember to buy ice cream to stuff them with before you spoon the warm chocolate sauce over the top!

SPECIAL EQUIPMENT 2 MEDIUM SAUCEPANS; STAND MIXER; 2 PARCHMENT PAPER-LINED BAKING SHEETS

8 tablespoons (120 g) unsalted
   butter, room temperature

½ cup (120 ml) milk

½ cup (120 ml) water

1 teaspoon vanilla extract

½ teaspoon almond extract

1½ tablespoons sugar

½ teaspoon salt

1 cup (120 g) all-purpose flour

3 large eggs, room temperature

ice cream

PREP

Preheat oven to 425° F (220° C).

COOK

In a saucepan, slowly melt the butter in the milk and water. Add the vanilla, almond extract, sugar, and salt and whisk to blend. Bring to a boil, reduce the heat to medium, and add the flour. Stir with a wooden spoon and cook just until the dough starts to pull away from the sides and forms a smooth ball.

Scrape the dough into the bowl of the stand mixer and cool down to room temperature then beat for 30 seconds on medium speed. Add 1 egg and beat until combined then add the other eggs, one by one, beating after each addition until you have a thick, glossy dough.

At this point, you can use a pastry bag or scoop the dough into a plastic bag and cut a corner to form perfect round balls on the baking sheet. Or you can use 2 large spoons to form balls of the dough on the

baking sheet, about 1 inch apart, until all the dough is used. Remember that you will be stuffing them with ice cream, so make them big enough to hold at least a tablespoonful.

Brush the tops with a little bit of water to round them out, and bake for 15 minutes. Rotate the baking sheets and make a tiny slit in the sides of each puff. Bake for another 5–10 minutes. Before turning off the oven, slice one in half to make sure they are dried out inside. If not, cook for another 5–10 minutes and check again. The puffs should be firm and sound hollow when gently tapped. When done, leave them in the oven, turn off the heat, and with a cake tester or needle, pierce the puffs a couple of times. Allow them to stay in the oven with the door slightly ajar until they are completely cool.

To serve, slice the balls in half, scoop ice cream into the bottom halves, top with their lids and drape warm chocolate sauce over the top.

DARK CHOCOLATE SAUCE

1 cup (240 ml) heavy cream

1 teaspoon vanilla extract

1 (12-ounce / 340-g) bag
   semisweet chocolate morsels

COOK

In a saucepan, bring the cream and vanilla just to a boil, remove from the heat, add the chocolate, and stir until melted, smooth, and dark.

IDEAS AND SUBSTITUTIONS

Tuck a slice of strawberry inside each puff, add some ice cream, put its top on, and simply dust with powdered sugar or a dollop of whipped cream.

CREAM-TOPPED APPLE TART

Tarte aux Pommes à la Normande SERVES 8

This was one of the recipes Madame, who lived up the hill from me in Provence, taught me. Her mother was from Normandy. From a fading card with handwritten notes, she'd read the instructions out loud as we cooked. When our work was done, we'd sit and count the minutes until our tart was ready to come out of the oven, having set the table with two plates and forks. We always had a slice right away then saved the rest for Monsieur's dinner.

SPECIAL EQUIPMENT FOOD PROCESSOR; ROLLING PIN; 9-INCH (23-CM) TART PAN WITH REMOVABLE BOTTOM OR PIE PLATE; PARCHMENT PAPER; BAKING BEANS OR RICE TO USE AS WEIGHTS

Pastry

1 1/2 cups (180 g) all-purpose flour

1/4 teaspoon salt

1 1/2 teaspoons ground cinnamon

1/2 teaspoon freshly ground nutmeg

2 tablespoons (30 ml) plus 2 teaspoons (10 ml) cold water

2 tablespoons (30 ml) apple brandy or Calvados

1 teaspoon vanilla extract

1/2 cup (1 stick / 120 g) unsalted butter, chilled

1 large egg yolk, room temperature

Filling

6 Granny Smith apples (about 2 pounds / about 900 g)

3 tablespoons (45 g) sweet butter, room temperature

1 cup (240 ml) heavy cream, room temperature

2 large eggs, room temperature

1 teaspoon vanilla extract

1 tablespoon (15 ml) plus 2 teaspoons (10 ml) apple brandy or Calvados

6 tablespoons (75 g) sugar, divided

1 teaspoon ground cinnamon

powdered sugar

PREP FOR PASTRY

Sift together the flour, salt, cinnamon, and nutmeg. In a small bowl, mix together the water, apple brandy, and vanilla.

COOK

Pastry

In the food processor, slice in the butter, add the egg yolk and water mixture, pulse a few times, and process for 6 seconds. Spoon in the flour mixture and process until mixed but not forming a ball. Scoop out onto a large piece of plastic wrap and form a ball then press into a disk and refrigerate for 1 hour.

On a clean, floured work surface, roll out the dough a little bigger than your tart pan, place the pan on the dough, and cut all the way around 1 inch (2.5 cm) larger than the pan. Lift the pan off the dough and place the dough inside the pan, pressing gently down around the edges. Crimp decoratively, leaving the dough slightly higher than the edges. Prick the bottom with a fork a few times and refrigerate the dough for 35 minutes.

continued >

Preheat the oven to 400° F (200° C).

When you are ready to bake the pastry, line it with wax paper, weigh it down with the baking beans or rice, and bake for 11 minutes. Remove the weights and parchment paper and bake for 5 minutes, or until golden brown. Remove and cool to room temperature.

Filling

Peel, core, and slice the apples in half. Either push them through the slicing disk in your food processor, slice thinly on a mandolin, or very thinly slice by hand with a knife. Arrange around and around the pastry in circles, overlapping slices. Dot with the butter and bake for 15 minutes.

While it is baking, whisk the cream, eggs, vanilla, apple brandy, 4 tablespoons (50 g) sugar, and cinnamon together. Pour over the apples in the tart, sprinkle with remaining sugar, return to the oven, and bake for 25–30 minutes, until the top is golden brown. Remove from the oven and cool to room temperature. I like to very lightly dust with a little powdered sugar over the top.

IDEAS AND SUBSTITUTIONS

In a pinch, use a store bought pie crust and, if you don't have Calvados, substitute brandy or cognac. Pears or plums also work very well in this tart.

RUM-SOAKED ALMOND CAKE FROM NANTES

Gâteau Nantais SERVES 6

I was so taken by the description of this extraordinarily simple one-layer glazed almond rum cake, which is a specialty of the city of Nantes in the northwest of France, and inspired by the recipe for it from Jamie Schler, who lives there and writes the blog, "Life's A Feast," that I've now made it many, many times. I've followed the spirit of Jamie's recipe, although I've changed it in a few ways. Households in Nantes slice it thinly, while in my house, we slice huge portions and devour it greedily with tea in the afternoon or with coffee after dinner.

SPECIAL EQUIPMENT 9-INCH (23-CM) CAKE PAN; PARCHMENT PAPER; STAND MIXER

Cake

1 cup (240 g) salted butter, room temperature, plus more for the cake pan

¾ cup (150 g) sugar

6 large eggs, room temperature

5 teaspoons (25 ml) almond extract

2 tablespoons (30 ml) dark rum, plus ¼ cup (60 ml), divided

⅔ cup (80 g) flour

2 cups (220 g) almond meal (Bob's Red Mill)

Glaze

1½ cups (190 g) powdered sugar

3 to 4 tablespoons (45 to 60 ml) rum

PREP

Generously butter the cake pan. Cut a circle of parchment paper, place in the bottom of the cake pan, and butter the circle.

Preheat oven to 350° F (180° C).

COOK

Cake

In the stand mixer, beat the butter and sugar until pale and fluffy. Beat in the eggs, one by one, until light and fluffy. Add the almond extract and 2 tablespoons (30 ml) rum and beat to mix. Add the flour and almond meal and beat until just blended.

Scrape the batter into the cake pan and bake for 25–30 minutes. Unmold cake onto a cooling rack and immediately pour ¼ cup (60 ml) rum over the top of the cake. Let the cake completely cool before glazing.

Glaze

Place a piece of parchment paper under the cooling rack to catch any glaze that falls. Whisk the powdered sugar with rum until smooth. Pour the glaze over the top and down the sides of the cake and spread with a spatula. Allow to rest for 30 minutes before serving.

IDEAS AND SUBSTITUTIONS

This dense rum-soaked cake is even better the next day and will last about 1 week. If you bake it in a square pan, cut it into small squares and glaze each square. They make wonderful small bites for parties or served on the saucer next to a cup of after-dinner coffee.

MACARON COOKIES FROM NANCY

Les Macarons de Nancy MAKES 15 COOKIES

At the bakery, Maison des Soeurs Macarons in Nancy, the original secret recipe for almond cookies, created and sold by two nuns to support themselves after the French Revolution, is still used. These are considered real macaron cookies, appearing long before the Parisian rainbow-of-colors version that has become so popular. In 1952, the city of Nancy designated the street where they made their cookies in honor of the nuns, announcing that theirs were the "veritable Macaron de Nancy" (authentic macaron cookies). Since then it has become a gastronomic destination just for these cookies.

This is the kind of cookie you dream of coming home to. They are soft in the center, yet a bit crispy on the outside—rather than looking perfect, they look homemade.

The good nuns' cookies were, many believe, made only with ground almonds, sugar, and egg whites—so I have stayed as close to their idea as possible.

SPECIAL EQUIPMENT FOOD PROCESSOR; 2 BAKING SHEETS LINED WITH PARCHMENT PAPER

½ cup (60 g) almond slivers

¾ cup (85 g) almond flour or meal (Bob's Red Mill)

¾ cup (150 g) sugar

2 large egg whites, room temperature

1 teaspoon almond extract

PREP

Preheat oven to 350° F (180° C).

COOK

In the food processor, process all ingredients until you have a paste.

Use a tablespoon of the paste for each cookie and space them out on the baking sheets with some room in between. With wet fingers, gently tap the cookies on the top to round them, though not to flatten them, and bake for 14–15 minutes, until they just barely turn golden around the edges with the tops still pale. Cool completely before serving.

IDEAS AND SUBSTITUTIONS

You can also make them as close in size as possible and sandwich a filling in between two of them. Or you can dust them with powdered sugar once they are cool.

SLIGHTLY LEMON POUND CAKE WITH STRAWBERRY RHUBARB COMPOTE AND WHIPPED CREAM

Quatre-Quarts au Citron, Compote de Fraises et Rhubarbe, Crème Chantilly SERVES 8

Every supermarket in France sells quatre-quarts, *a simple pound cake made with four main ingredients, all the same weight. When making it at home, I change the ingredients a little and add a hint of lemon. It pairs beautifully with a slightly tart spring compote of strawberries and rhubarb, although you can prepare a fruit compote with any seasonal fruits. Topped with a cloud of lightly whipped vanilla cream, it becomes ethereal.*

SPECIAL EQUIPMENT 9 X 5-INCH (23 X 13-CM) LOAF PAN; STAND MIXER OR LARGE BOWL WITH HAND-HELD ELECTRIC MIXER; MEDIUM SAUCEPAN WITH LID

Cake

1 cup (2 sticks / 240 g) salted butter, room temperature, plus extra for loaf pan

2½ cups (300 g) all-purpose flour

1 teaspoon baking powder

¼ teaspoon salt

¼ cup (60 ml) half-and-half, room temperature

1½ teaspoons lemon extract

1 cup (200 g) sugar

5 large eggs, room temperature

Compote

16 ounces (450 g) rhubarb, cut into chunks

1 tablespoon (15 ml) water

4 tablespoons (50 g) sugar

¼ teaspoon vanilla extract

8 ounces (225 g) strawberries, hulled and thickly sliced

Chantilly

2 cups (480 ml) heavy cream, chilled

1 teaspoon vanilla extract

½ teaspoon almond extract

3 tablespoons (30 g) superfine sugar

PREP FOR CAKE

Generously butter loaf pan. Sift together flour, baking powder, and salt. Combine half-and-half and lemon extract.

Preheat oven to 300° F (150° C).

COOK

Cake

In the bowl of the stand mixer, beat butter until pale and fluffy. Gradually add sugar while the machine is running. Continue to beat for 2 minutes. Scrape down the bowl and add eggs, one by one, beating after each addition, just enough to mix.

Add the sifted ingredients alternately with the half-and-half mixture, ending with the dry ingredients. Beat until combined.

Pour into the loaf pan, place in the oven, and bake for 1 hour and 20–30 minutes, until golden and a cake tester comes out clean. Cool completely before slicing.

Compote

Place the rhubarb in the saucepan with the water, sugar, and vanilla. Cover and cook on medium-low, stirring often, until the rhubarb is soft, about 12 minutes. Add the strawberries and cook another 5 minutes. Mix well with a fork and cool to room temperature.

Chantilly

In the stand mixer, place the cream, vanilla, almond extract, and sugar and beat until it begins to take shape as soft whipped cream. Transfer to a bowl, cover, and refrigerate until ready to use.

To serve, place a slice of cake on each plate, spoon the compote over half of it, and mound the Chantilly on top of the compote.

IDEAS AND SUGGESTIONS

I like to drizzle a little orange liqueur (Cointreau or Grand Marnier) over the pound cake slices before serving, or add a little when I whip the Chantilly cream.

Don't refrigerate the cake as it will harden. Keep it covered at room temperature.

WALNUT TART IN WALNUT PASTRY

Tarte aux Noix SERVES 8

Groves of walnut trees thrive in the Périgord region in southwest France, which is where this tart originates.
The crust should chill for at least 2 hours before you bake it, or prepare it the day before and bake it the next day. I make
this tart with walnuts in three ways: in the crust, in the filling, and topping the sugar glaze before slicing and serving it.

SPECIAL EQUIPMENT 9-INCH (23-CM) FLUTED TART PAN WITH REMOVABLE BOTTOM; FOOD PROCESSOR; ROLLING PIN; PARCHMENT PAPER; BAKING BEANS OR RICE TO USE AS WEIGHTS; SAUCEPAN

Pastry

½ cup (1 stick / 120 g) unsalted butter, chilled, plus extra for tart pan

1½ cups (180 g) all-purpose flour

4 tablespoons (50 g) sugar

¼ teaspoon salt

1½ teaspoons ground cinnamon

¼ cup (30 g) walnuts

1 teaspoon vanilla extract

1 large egg, room temperature

4 to 5 tablespoons (60 to 75 ml) cold water

Filling

2 cups (240 g) walnuts

1¼ cups (300 ml) half-and-half

6 tablespoons (90 ml) honey

1 tablespoon sugar

1½ teaspoons vanilla extract

1 tablespoon butter

3 large eggs

Glaze

1 cup (125 g) powdered sugar

3 tablespoons (45 ml) dark rum or brandy (or water)

1 cup (120 g) walnuts, coarsely chopped

PREP

Slice butter and place on a plate in the refrigerator until ready to use. Butter the tart pan.

COOK

Pastry

Put the flour, sugar, salt, cinnamon, and walnuts in the food processor and process until it looks like sand. Pour it into a bowl.

Put the butter, vanilla, egg, and water in the food processor and process for 3 seconds. Pour the flour mixture back into the food processor and process until blended, but not until it forms a ball. Scoop everything out onto a large piece of plastic wrap, fold

it over, and use your fingers to form a ball of dough. Flatten it into a disk and place in the refrigerator at least 2 hours or overnight.

On a clean, lightly floured work surface, roll out the disk of dough to about 1 inch larger than the tart pan. Fit the rolled out dough into the pan, pressing gently into the corners, and trim to overhang to about ½ inch (1.27 cm) higher than the tart pan. Roll the excess dough over all the way around into a cord and crimp with your fingers. With a fork, prick the dough in several places and then place in the refrigerator for 40 minutes.

Preheat the oven to 400° F (200° C).

continued >

When you are ready to bake the crust, lay a piece of parchment paper in the bottom and weigh it down with baking beans or rice. Bake for 11 minutes, remove the weights and parchment paper, and bake an additional 5–7 minutes, or until it is golden. Cool to room temperature.

Reduce the oven temperature to 350° F (180° C).

Filling

In the bowl of the food processor, add the walnuts and process 10 seconds until they are large granules.

In the saucepan, bring the half-and-half, honey, sugar, and vanilla just to a boil. Whisk in the butter until well combined then take off the heat.

Beat the eggs in a large bowl. Pour in a little of the hot milk mixture and whisk. Pour in the rest and whisk well. Pour in the walnuts and stir to mix. Scoop into the pastry crust and bake for 35–40 minutes, until the custard is set. Remove from the oven and cool to room temperature then unmold the tart onto a serving plate.

Glaze

Whisk the powdered sugar with the rum and pour over the top of the tart, tilting the tart to spread it and allowing any excess to drip off. Decorate with the chopped walnuts.

IDEAS AND SUBSTITUTIONS

In a pinch, use a premade all butter frozen pie crust. It saves time, although does not compare with making your own pastry crust.

NOEL YULE LOG

Bûche de Noël MAKES 2 LOGS SERVING 12–14

French villages at Christmastime are strewn with lights in the shape of star bursts and meteors that at night create a winter wonderland. A Christmas tree is the main decoration in town squares, while churches are outlined with lights against the night sky. Often there is a Christmas market populated with timber chalet stalls selling crafts, gifts, holiday foods, and mugs of steaming hot mulled wine you can drink while you walk around and shop.

Inside village houses, reindeer, twig trees, and pinecones create a natural setting for a Christmas feast to appear, the crowning glory being the dessert, a Bûche de Noël.

French families, for the most part, buy theirs as the pastry shops make fabulous ones for the holidays. You can follow these directions to make your own Bûche de Noël to celebrate your Christmas—the French way.

SPECIAL EQUIPMENT PARCHMENT PAPER; 11 X 17-INCH (28 X 43-CM) JELLY ROLL BAKING PAN; HAND-HELD ELECTRIC MIXER; FOOD PROCESSOR; DISH TOWEL LARGER THAN THE JELLY ROLL PAN; ALUMINUM FOIL; STAND MIXER; BAKING SHEET

Cake

3 large eggs, room temperature

¾ cup (90 g) cake flour

1½ teaspoons baking powder

¼ teaspoon salt

½ cup (100 g) sugar

1 teaspoon vanilla extract

½ teaspoon almond extract

1 tablespoon (15 ml) water plus 1½ teaspoons

powdered sugar

Filling

10 tablespoons (150 g) unsalted butter, softened

2 to 3 cups (225 to 350 g) powdered sugar, divided

1 cup (120 g) unsweetened cocoa

½ cup (120 ml) milk

1 tablespoon espresso powder

Frosting

5 tablespoons (75 g) unsalted butter, softened

2 tablespoons espresso powder

½ cup (60 g) unsweetened cocoa

4 to 5 cups (500 to 600 g) powdered sugar

½ cup (120 ml) milk

PREP FOR CAKE

Cut parchment paper to extend beyond the edges of the jelly roll pan by 1 inch (2.5 cm). Butter the paper, lightly flour, shake off any excess, and fit into the jelly roll pan.

Separate the eggs into yolks and whites. Sift flour, baking powder, and salt together.

Preheat the oven to 375° F (190° C).

COOK

Cake

Place the egg whites in a mixing bowl and, with the hand mixer, beat until almost stiff. In the food processor, place the egg yolks, sugar, vanilla, almond extract, and water and process for 45 seconds. Spoon the flour mixture into the food processor then spoon in the beaten egg whites. Pulse

continued >

2 times, scrape down the sides, and pulse again 3–4 times, just until blended. You may see a bit of egg white, but that is fine.

Scoop everything onto the jelly roll pan and spread out evenly to cover the pan. Place in the oven and bake for 10–14 minutes, until golden on top, a toothpick in the center comes out clean, and the edges are beginning to pull away from the pan. Take out of the oven and immediately sieve powdered sugar all over the top of the cake. Cover with parchment paper and the dish towel and invert onto a kitchen counter or table. Cool the cake for 2 minutes then peel off the paper from the top, generously dust with powdered sugar, and invert onto a piece of aluminum foil larger than the cake. At this point I slice off the crisp edges, to produce an even rectangle, then starting from one of the short sides, use the foil to roll the cake into a spiral.

Filling

In the bowl of the stand mixer, beat the butter until pale and fluffy. Add 1 cup (125 g) of powdered sugar and the cocoa and beat until blended, and then add a little of the milk and beat again. Keep alternating powdered sugar and milk until the filling is smooth and spreadable. Beat in the espresso powder.

Unroll the cake, spread the filling over the cake, except for 1 inch (2.5 cm) at the short ends, and then use the foil to help firmly roll the cake into a log shape, beginning with the short side, but not so tightly that the cake breaks. Slice off 1 inch (2.5 cm) from each of the short ends.

Transfer the log to the baking sheet, cover, and refrigerate for at least 30 minutes.

Frosting

Beat the butter until pale and fluffy. Add the espresso powder, cocoa, and a little powdered sugar and beat to blend. Add in some milk and beat. Begin alternating powdered sugar and milk until the frosting is smooth and spreadable.

Cut the log in half. Frost the outside of the rolls. The rougher it looks the better. Run a fork over the logs from one end to the other to approximate bark. Sieve a little powdered sugar around the serving platter to look like snow.

IDEAS AND SUBSTITUTIONS

There are so many things you can do with this basic recipe. Change the chocolate filling to vanilla or raspberry. Spread the cake with warmed jam before filling and rolling. Decorate with tiny chocolates, cookies, or holiday ornaments that could be fairy folk, deer, or pine trees. Make an elegant shiny frosting instead of this more rustic one. Once you have the roll technique in hand, you can go wherever your imagination takes you for decorating your *Bûche de Noël*.

RASPBERRY-ALMOND MINI-CAKES

Financiers aux Framboises MAKES 24

Miniature pink rectangular cakes were lined up in a white cardboard box behind a stall I shop at in an open-air market. "Financiers?" I asked, hoping they were for sale. "Oui, Madame!"

I bought six and ate three right away. They were moist and light and flavored with fresh raspberries yet having a pronounced almond flavor. After that first introduction, I decided to learn how to make them at home. The secret, I discovered, was the use of beurre noisette, or brown butter.

I bought both a proper Financier baking pan with rectangular molds, as well as a silicon one. If you don't have one, use mini-muffin baking tins.

SPECIAL EQUIPMENT 2 MINI-MUFFIN TINS (24 MUFFINS IN TOTAL); FOOD PROCESSOR; SAUCEPAN

½ cup (1 stick / 120 g) unsalted butter, softened, plus enough to grease your tins

½ cup (70 g) fresh raspberries

1 cup (120 g) slivered almonds

5 large egg whites, room temperature

2 teaspoons almond extract

½ teaspoon vanilla extract

½ cup (60 g) all-purpose flour

1¼ cups (160 g) sifted powdered sugar

¼ teaspoon baking powder

pinch of salt

PREP

Preheat oven to 400° F (200° C). Grease the tins with butter and refrigerate. Purée the raspberries in the food processor.

COOK

Melt the butter in the saucepan over medium-low heat, bring to a boil, and without disturbing it, let boil, swirling once in a while, until it takes on a golden brown color. You'll notice the foam disappear and the smell of hazelnuts as the butter browns. This is your beurre noisette. Remove from the heat as soon as it reaches a light, not too dark, brown color, about 5 minutes. Cool to room temperature.

In the food processor, process the almonds until it looks like fine sand. In a small bowl, lightly whisk egg whites with the almond extract and vanilla.

Transfer the ground almonds into a large bowl, add the flour, powdered sugar, baking powder, salt, egg white mixture, browned butter, and raspberries. Whisk to barely combine. Spoon into tins and bake 12 minutes until golden brown then turn out onto a wire rack to cool.

IDEAS AND SUGGESTIONS

Try these using pistachios or hazelnuts and top them with a drizzle of warm chocolate, press one raspberry in the top of each before baking, or sprinkle them with powdered sugar.

BRIE MELTED IN BOX WITH BROWN SUGAR FOR TWO

Brie Rôti au Sucre Roux, pour Deux SERVES 2

What better way to end my cookbook than with a final recipe for a dessert meant for two? After all, the ultimate comfort is being able to share delicious food with someone you love. So pick up your spoons and dip into this sublime treat that can be ready in minutes.

SPECIAL EQUIPMENT BAKING SHEET OR BAKING DISH

1 (8-ounce / 230-g) Brie cheese in its box, room temperature

1 tablespoon dark brown sugar

1 baguette, sliced or crackers

PREP

Preheat oven to 350° F (180° C).

Take the Brie out of its box, remove the wrapper, slice off just the top rind, and put the cheese back in its box without its cover.

COOK

Place the box on the baking sheet, sprinkle the cheese evenly with brown sugar, and bake for 6–10 minutes, or until oozy.

Serve on one plate with two spoons and slices of crusty bread or crackers nearby.

IDEAS AND SUBSTITUTIONS

You can add any kind of jam, fruit compote, or honey and walnuts to the interior center of the cheese.

ACKNOWLEDGMENTS

My thanks to managing editor Madge Baird, for encouraging me to do this project; to my wonderful editor, Michelle Branson, for her support and keen eye; to Sheryl Dickert for her inspired design; and to the entire team at Gibbs Smith for their professionalism and eagerness to create a beautiful book.

To Deborah Ritchken, my agent, special thanks for going above and beyond the call of duty, for being eternally enthusiastic, and for always understanding and taking such good care of me. You are amazing and I am very grateful for everything that you do.

To Steven Rothfeld, world-class photographer, my heartfelt thanks for signing on for another cookbook photo shoot with me. We are, again, equal partners in this opus.

Thank you to my good friend, French cookbook author, Hélène Lautier, who lives in Cannes and who translated titles and combed the manuscript to make sure all French wording was proper.

To my blog followers and recipe testers, especially to those who repeatedly tested and tasted and commented and suggested—thank you!!! Thanks especially to Carl De Prima, Barbara Michelson, Katrina Hall, Deborah Ritchken, and Sandy Taylor. Thank you Beth Marinello, for not only recipe testing, but for convincing me to write a chapter about doing brunch the French way!

To dear Prudence May Plusch, a huge thank you for generously taking my crew into your beautiful home for our photo shoot, for sharing treasured antiques, and for graciousness and hospitality that was extraordinary and very appreciated by us all. To Judith May Zouck, a big hug and thank you for providing hospitality, conviviality, and friendship to my crew as well.

Huge thanks to Richard M. Plusch Antiques in North Conway, New Hampshire, for graciously providing antiques and linens for the photo shoot.

To my treasured friends who are always there for me, offering encouragement and moral support: Joanie and Jeremy Frost, Blandine Beaulieu, Grove Hafela, the Fairfield Road tasters, Foster Thalheimer, Holly Herrick, Jennifer Cartmell (my PR coordinator and friend), Jane Cartmell, Helen De Prima, Susan Laughlin, Betsy Callas, Ombretta Lanza, Giovanni Agusta, Rachel Malé, Amy Markus, Chef Luca Paris, and George Sheinberg—thank you. And thanks to Spike, Piper, and Fricky for their patience waiting for a walk between recipe tests and their welcoming tails wagging at the end of the day.

To Bill Cochrane, my love always. *

INDEX